The 5 Skills

Core Competencies for Educators and Youth Workers

JT (Jerry) Fest

ISBN-13: 978-1721729203
ISBN-10: 1721729208

DEDICATION

This book is dedicated to you, the youth worker; in whatever capacity you may be working with young people. You endure long hours, low pay, and minimal gratitude while helping young people become their best selves. I hope this book helps you as you help others, and I offer my most sincere thanks and admiration for the work that you do.

I am also grateful to Peter Linnell, for checking my math.

CONTENTS

INTRODUCTION

What do we mean by "core competencies?" The concept of core competencies was first introduced in an article published in 1990 in the Harvard Business Review. Written by C.K. Prahalad and Gary Hamel, the article described core competencies as the main strengths or strategic advantages of a business. While a business might expand into or demonstrate other competencies as well, its "core competencies" are what gives the business its competitive advantage.

This concept grew into recognition of individual core competencies, that is, the skills, knowledge, and attributes possessed by an individual that gives them a competitive advantage in their field. While an individual in any profession will need to develop a broad set of skills and abilities, core competencies refers to the skills or abilities that one *must* have to adequately perform in their chosen profession; and these competencies will be different depending on one's profession.

In the 1990's and early 2000's as the Positive Youth Development (PYD) approach[1] gained popularity, particularly among organizations working with runaway and street-dependent youth, many efforts were made to define the core competencies of a PYD youth worker. What resulted was extensive lists of dozens of skills that in my mind missed the point entirely. "Core competency" is not

---

[1] This approach is described in greater detail in my book The Winning Hand Workbook; Positive Youth Development in 6 Easy Lessons.

1

a reference to everything you need to know how to do; it is not a list of every skill and ability that must be mastered; rather, it is a reference to the few 'core' things that one *has* to master or their performance will be negatively impacted, no matter how many other skills and abilities they have.

In my earlier book "Street Culture 2.0: An Epistemology of Street Dependent Youth," I included an introduction to Positive Youth Development and followed that up with "The Winning Hand Workbook, Positive Youth Development in 6 Easy Lessons." In each of those works I made the case that it was impossible to develop a universal list of core competencies since PYD was an *approach*, not a profession. The core competencies needed to be a teacher using the PYD approach will be different from those of a juvenile probation officer or a street outreach worker, so I instead described the specific skills necessary to promote youth involvement and participation (a key element of the PYD approach).

This book is an attempt to answer a broader question; what are the core competencies needed to be an effective youth worker? Regardless of the job one does, the approach one uses, or the program model in which one functions, is there a set of "core" skills or competences one can master that will improve one's work and outcomes and, without which, performance will suffer?

I say yes, though my answer is based on my personal experience derived from 10 years of direct service work; 21 years of program development, management, and supervision; and 17 years of training and consultation on the international level. I present this answer to both the new and the experienced youth worker with the assurance that if you can master the 5 specific skills in this book and make them your "core competencies" upon which all of your other knowledge, skills, and abilities rest, you will find that your relationships with youth clients will be easier, your work with them will be more effective, and your outcomes will improve. It is to that end that this book describes a youth worker's core competencies; which I call "The 5 Skills."

Throughout this book I refer to "teachers, juvenile probation officers, and street outreach workers." This is intended simply to show application to a diversity of youth work settings, not to limit the skills to application in those settings only. If you are a professional or para-professional who is working with young people in any capacity, these 5 skills are applicable to the work you do.

ONE OF FIVE
It Starts with Respect

I put this skill first for a reason. Even if you get nothing else out of this book, I believe that you will have greater success with young people if you master this skill, as it is the foundation for all youth work. But, in order to master the skill of respect, we need to understand what it is.

What do we mean by respect?

Respect (as a noun) is defined as a *feeling of deep admiration for someone or something elicited by their abilities, qualities, or achievements.* This definition may be applicable to our work with young people; teachers may respect a student's aptitude for learning; a probation officer may respect a probationer's ability to adapt to the terms of their probation; and a street outreach worker may respect a street youth's ability to survive. But it isn't *always* applicable to our work, as we arguably may not have a *feeling of deep admiration* for a lack of knowledge, behavior that resulted in adjudication and probation, or what a street-dependent youth has to do to survive. And this is where the whole issue of respect gets muddied and difficult for workers to practice, because respect is generally thought of as a noun; something that we *have* for someone or something. But when we're discussing respect as a youth work *skill*, we're not using it as a noun, we're using it as a *verb*.

Respect as a verb

When we consider respect as a verb rather than as a noun, we've changed the conversation from something we *have*, to something we *do*. Instead of talking about *deep admiration for abilities, qualities, or achievements*, we are talking about *due regard for the feelings, rights, or traditions of others*. It is possible to have *deep admiration* and *due regard* at the same time, but it is by no means required to have both. We can find someone's beliefs and behaviors abhorrent, while simultaneously having due regard for their feelings, rights and traditions. It is neither accepting nor condoning to treat someone with respect, nor is it necessary to have respect for their *abilities, qualities, or achievements* to do so. But to be helpful to young people, it is necessary to *treat* them with respect (verb), regardless of whether or not we feel that they are *deserving* of our respect (noun).

Why is respect important?

Respect is not something that can be neutral. As a verb, it is an action, which means that it is either something that we are doing, or *not* doing. In other words, if we are not treating someone with respect (due regard), then we are by default treating them *disrespectfully*. The definition of disrespect is *to regard or treat with contempt or rudeness*. In any engagement we have with other human beings, we have only two options; to treat them respectfully, or to be rude. Clearly, when our goal is to educate or to reduce or heal trauma and foster resilience, having someone experience our treatment of them as contemptuous or rude does not further that goal. Therefore, to be successful in our efforts to be of service to young people, we must actively treat them with respect (verb), regardless of whether or not we actually have respect (noun) for them.

What is due regard?

There is a legal definition for *due regard*. It means to give *fair consideration* and *sufficient attention to*. In the legal world, it requires that fair consideration and sufficient attention be given to *all* of the facts in a case. In the sense of treating someone with respect, it means that we are giving due regard, that is, fair consideration and sufficient attention, to their *feelings, rights, or traditions*. It means that, regardless of the nature of the relationship; be it education in a mandated circumstance (as with most teachers, though voluntary educational environments exist), authority in a statutory circumstance (as with a probation officer), or support in a voluntary circumstance (as with a street outreach worker); we are tempering our treatment of them and actions toward them with consideration of how our treatment impacts their feelings, rights, or traditions. It is antithetical to a helping relationship to intentionally manipulate or disregard someone's feelings, or to ignore or violate their rights, or to dismiss or be ignorant of their traditions.

What does treating respectfully look like?

If you're reading this, you are most likely a professional in education, criminal justice, social service, or some other youth work field. As a professional you are, or should be, aware of your actions and responses and how they impact those in your care. Just as the best way to build trust is to be trustworthy, the best way to practice respect is to treat others respectfully, which is something you already know how to do, and should be self-aware enough to recognize when you're not doing it. But for guidance, some of the essential elements of acting respectfully include that:

1. We are *honest*: We do not lie, deceive, or manipulate. We share relevant information. If we make a mistake, we admit it, take responsibility for our actions, and apologize. If there are reasons why we can't be openly honest and share information (confidentiality or other reasons), we acknowledge that and share the reasons why we can't share the information.

2. We are *fair*: We don't make assumptions. We genuinely listen to understand, and we seek the other's perspective before reaching a conclusion. We hold ourselves and young people accountable but avoid punishment; consequences are logical and natural results of actions taken.

3. We are *kind*: We never intentionally embarrass, ridicule, insult, dismiss, or make fun of young people. Criticism is always

constructive, and we compliment at least as much, preferable more, than we constructively criticize. We avoid sarcasm, as sarcasm is often misunderstood or misinterpreted by young people, particularly so if we are in a position of authority over them. This does not mean that we can't have fun and joke around with young people; but it does mean that we are aware of how our words and actions are being received, and we never joke with them at their expense.

4. We are *considerate*: We acknowledge boundaries, personal space, and feelings, and we never violate or disregard feelings without just cause. Should we have just cause, we do so without malice and explain what we are doing and why. We use words like "please" and "thank you," and we pay attention to and address legitimate concerns and needs.

5. We are *reliable*: We don't make promises that we can't keep, and we follow through with what we say we'll do. We keep appointments and we show up (and end) on time. We are consistent in our words and actions.

6. We are *concerned*: We take and demonstrate genuine interest in the young person's perspectives, abilities, and life. We not only try to help them become the best they can be, we are interested in and concerned about who they are *now*.

These six essential elements are not the be all and end all of treating others respectfully, but they are good guideposts for examining our behavior in the "heat of the moment." It's a good checklist to review in your head when you're working with young people, particularly when emotions are high and situations are difficult. It is always a good idea to ask yourself; am I practicing *honesty, fairness, kindness, consideration, reliability, and concern*? Of course, an even easier test is to ask yourself, *how would I feel if someone was talking to or treating me the way I'm talking to or treating this young person*? If the answer is anything other than *understood, supported*, and *cared about*, stop what you're doing, and do something else.

What if I'm not being treated respectfully?

Sorry, but that's not even relevant. Treating young people respectfully is something that *we* do; it is a *skill* that we practice, and it is completely unrelated to whether or not it is reciprocal. Of course, we *respond* to disrespectful treatment; it is not something that we ignore; but our response is given *respectfully*. We do not meet disrespect with disrespect; we role model the behavior we seek. Most of us are familiar with the de-escalation technique of remaining calm and speaking softly in response to people who are agitated and speaking loudly. They will eventually begin to mirror our behavior and calm themselves. In the same way, respond respectfully to disrespect and young people will eventually begin to mirror respectful responses.

Isn't part of our job to teach respect?

Yes, if we're talking about a verb. No, if we're talking about a noun. But any good teacher will tell you that you don't teach by command, you teach by example and engagement. We teach respect as a verb by consistently practicing respect, and the moment we stop practicing respect … we get overwhelmed, or frustrated, or angry … and respond to disrespect with disrespect, we teach the exact opposite of the behavior we seek. This is one of the main reasons why consistently practicing respect is one of the five most important skills, because by your behavior toward young people you are always teaching; and if you're not teaching respect, you're teaching disrespect.

As for teaching respect as a noun; that is, teaching a young person to have respect for people or things, the fact is that respect (noun) is not something that can be *taught*. It is, and always will be, something that needs to be *earned*. If we *demand* respect, what we actually get is either *resentment* that escalates negative behavior, or *fear* that we misinterpret as respect. We earn respect by being *honest, fair, kind, considerate, reliable, and concerned*. In other words, the way to earn respect (noun) is to practice respect (verb).

The first of the Five Skills is:

The ability to consistently treat young people in our care respectfully (verb); regardless of whether their behaviors, choices, and actions deserve our respect (noun), and regardless of whether they respect us, or are treating us respectfully. It is the consistent practice of *honesty, fairness, kindness, consideration, reliability, and concern* in all of our words and actions that constitutes respect.

TWO OF FIVE
'Tain't What You Do (It's the Way That You Do It)

We've know this ever since jazz musicians Melvin "Sy" Oliver and James "Trummy" Young put it to music, and it was first recorded back in 1939 by Ella Fitzgerald. At least, we've known the song. What we sometimes need to learn is just how important the theme of this song is to youth work. You might want to look it up on Youtube just to get the tune in your head, and whenever we are with a young person we should consider it to be our background music, because … as the lyrics go … *"that's what gets results."*

What is "what" we do?

We have job duties and responsibilities, and we are seeking certain outcomes for young people. *What* those things are depends on our employment. We may be a teacher responsible for education and socialization. We may be a juvenile probation officer responsible for safety and transformation. We may be a street outreach worker responsible for harm reduction and motivating change. Or we may be in one of a hundred other positions, statutory (public), non-statutory (private), or even as a volunteer . . . but the distinguishing characteristic of our work is that we spend time with young people with the goal of creating change. Our job duties and responsibilities and the outcomes that we seek constitute *what* we do. But *what* we do only defines the change that we seek; it does not motivate that change. Change is motivated by *how* we do *what* we do.

10

What is "how" we do it?

All work requires specific skills and abilities. When working with people, particularly young people, the skills and abilities employed are interpersonal ones. A mechanic requires no cooperation from the car to improve its performance, but a teacher cannot teach; a juvenile probation officer cannot keep a community safe; and a street outreach worker cannot connect a youth with higher services, without the volitional (willful) cooperation of the young person. This is a fact that is often under-recognized in youth work. We can *force* circumstances (we can make them go to school; we can place them in detention, we can initiate conversation on the street), but we can't force *outcomes*. All positive (and negative) outcomes are a result of a young person's volitional choices and decisions. As an early mentor of mine once told me, it doesn't matter if a young person has the *right* to do something, what matters is whether or not they have the *power* to do it. Young people do not have the *right* to skip school, or break the law, or leave home to live on our streets; but they have the *power* to do all three and focusing on their right is a moot point. Our only ability is the ability to *influence* their power and how they choose to use it. We do that not by controlling the young person, but by shaping the young person's experiences and environments. This is what is meant by *how* we do what we do; it is how a young person *experiences* what we practice. *How* we do *what* we do creates the experiences and environments that will influence a young person toward positive (or negative) outcomes. A quote by Maya Angelou is appropriate here: "I've learned that people will forget what you said, people will forget what you did, but people will never forget how you made them feel."

Don't overestimate our ability to influence

Let's say, for example, that we're a typical teacher who has a student for 1 grade year. In the United States, on average that's about 36 weeks, with about 19 hours per week of formal instruction, according to the National Center for Education Statistics. That's a total of 684 hours that we'll spend with that student annually.

Assume that the student sleeps an average of 8 hours per night.

Over the course of a 12-year education, that student will have 70,080 waking hours. The 684 hours we spend with that student ... that is, the time available to influence their actions and choices ... amounts to less than 0.01% of their waking hours. Even if we look at our ability to influence them within a single year of their life, they have 5,840 waking hours. Our 684 hours amounts to just over 1/10th of 1% of their time ... and that assumes that we're spending each of those 684 hours in meaningful interaction with that student. The reality is that those 684 hours are divided among the 15 to 30 or more students in our classroom.

When we look at other forms of youth work ... e.g., probation, street outreach, case management ... the numbers are even worse. According to the American Probation and Parole Association, a "high priority" case should receive 4 hours per month of supervision. Case management services receive a similar amount of time per case, and even programs where young people and adults interact more consistently (residential programs, drop-in services, etc.), an individual adult will only spend a few hours per week at best in significant contact with an individual young person. Even programs designed to be an influential adult in a young person's life, such as being a Big Brother or Sister, amount to only 3-5 hours per week of significant interaction. At the high end, that's an annual commitment of 260 hours, or less than 0.05% of a child's waking life.

Don't underestimate our ability to influence

Despite the limited percentage of a young person's time that any one person interacts with them, we can ... in fact we do ... have the ability for great influence. Young people are present-oriented, and their beliefs and behaviors are often shaped by "moments in time," and a single moment can have deep and long-lasting effects. The child who touches a hot stove will quickly conclude not to do that again, despite the fact that it was a single, brief event. In the same way, the child who comes to us for support on a day when we're just not at our best ... we had a fight with our spouse or we got chewed out by our supervisor, and we blow them off or don't fully give them our attention ... will quickly conclude not to do *that* again. This is the greatest challenge of youth work; in many ways, we don't get to have a bad day. Every moment that we are interacting with a young person is part of that precious, tiny percentage of time available to influence, and everything that we chose to say or do is a moment in time that can have deep and long-lasting effects on a young person … for better or for worse. Whether it's for better or for worse is determined by *how* the young person experiences us.

Treatment is just a clinical term for influence

Treatment techniques and plans are simply codified methods and blueprints for achieving certain outcomes. All youth work is a form of treatment, which in its most basic understanding is defined as *"the manner in which someone behaves toward or deals with someone or something."* Whether we are "treating" a young person for a lack of knowledge (as does a teacher), or for criminal behavior (as does a juvenile probation officer), or for a lack of basic needs and healthy coping skills (as does a street outreach worker), or any other work with young people, it all comes down to *how* treatment is being provided; that is, the manner in which we are behaving toward those we wish to influence. This should not be confused with treatment *techniques*, which, depending on *what* we do, may involve methods like Cooperative Learning, Cognitive Behavioral Therapy, Motivational Interviewing, or hundreds of other approaches (including the *What versus How* technique in Appendix A). But whatever technique we are using, its effectiveness will be determined by the manner in which we are behaving, which will likewise determine the manner in which young people respond to us. This is the very definition of a *relationship*; the manner in which two or more people regard and behave toward each other.

A treatment relationship has a name

The basis of all treatment is the relationship between treatment providers and those receiving treatment. It is within the context of this relationship that all treatment occurs. But "relationship" is a large category that includes many different forms of human interaction; some that are healthy, positive, and helpful; some that are unhealthy, negative, and harmful. In relationships where an adult is employed or volunteering to achieve positive outcomes with a young person, the healthy, positive, and helpful relationship that needs to be established is known as a *therapeutic alliance*. While this may sound "clinical" and is usually used in the context of a relationship between physical or mental healthcare professionals and their patients or clients, it is also the best way to describe the relationship needed between a professional or para-professional adult and a young person in order to be able to influence positive outcomes. The relationship itself may exist between a teacher and a student, or an officer and a probationer, or an outreach worker and a street-dependent youth; but it is a relationship based on a therapeutic alliance between a *helper* and a person being *helped*.

What defines a therapeutic alliance?

The definition of therapy is *treatment intended to heal or relieve a disorder*, and while "alliance" has many definitions, the definition referred to here is that of a *collaboration*. So, when we define a relationship as a therapeutic alliance, we are describing a *collaborative process* where the *manner in which* we *behave toward or deal with someone* is intended to *heal or relieve a disorder* (e.g., lack of knowledge, criminal behavior, street dependency). Since the goal of our treatment is to heal or relieve disorders, we need to understand what young people need in order to be healed or relieved.

The foundation for change

Regardless of the challenges a young person is facing, or the outcomes we are responsible for helping them to achieve, all young people have certain basic needs that act as a foundation for their ability to grow and mature into healthy adulthood. Ignore these basic needs and our ability to *heal or relieve* will be compromised. While different sources may define these needs differently, in terms of a therapeutic alliance we can say that these basic needs are the need *to feel safe*, the need *to trust*, and the need *to be seen* (that is, to be acknowledged as a unique individual with value). Regardless of *what* we are doing, addressing these basic needs is a critical aspect of *how* we are doing it. A child who does not feel *safe* cannot learn or advance to addressing psychological and self-actualization needs. A child who does not *trust* will not feel safe. And a child who does not feel *seen* will not be able to trust.

Fostering resilience in a therapeutic alliance

According to the basic tenets of Positive Youth Development, young people have an innate capacity for resilience which provides them with the ability to overcome and even benefit from negative experiences and circumstances. It is challenges that young people face in their lives and how they deal with them that defines who they become, and it is their innate capacity for resilience that enables them to grow and learn from adversity. But while resilience is an innate human capacity, the environment … that is, the surroundings or conditions in which we live and/or operate … serves to either foster or inhibit our innate capacity for resilience. When we live and/or operate in environments characterized by *risk factors* … negative influences in or lives such as neglect, violence, and various forms of abuse …. our capacity for resilience is inhibited. But when we are exposed to *protective factors* … caring and supportive relationships, high expectations, and meaningful participation . . . our innate capacity for resilience is fostered, and we become better able to deal with and overcome whatever challenges we are facing. A therapeutic alliance serves two goals. First, to provide a relationship in which a young person can feel safe, learn to trust, and be seen as a foundation for learning and addressing psychological and self-actualization needs; and second, a therapeutic alliance is an important part of creating a resilience-fostering environment.

How to do what we do

Creating a therapeutic alliance requires first establishing clear and mutually understood role definitions. A teacher and a student have a relationship, but their roles in that relationship are different and defined by the purpose of those roles. When roles aren't clear and mutually understood, neither party in the relationship is truly safe. If I see myself as your probation officer, but you see me as your friend, conflict is bound to occur, and the relationship will not be safe. The first step in establishing a therapeutic alliance is to ensure that both parties understand the nature of the alliance; that is, the role each party plays in the relationship and the goals (purpose) of the alliance.

The next step is establishing trust, defined as *the firm belief in the reliability of someone*. In other words, the greater one is able to predict or assume our actions and responses, the greater their trust in us. It is as simple and as complicated as being *transparent* and *consistent* in our behavior and actions. Transparency assures young people that they can trust in what is being said to them, and consistency assures that young people feel secure in their trust, as they know what to expect from us.

Finally, remember that we are establishing an *alliance*. It is a *collaboration*, and therefore both parties must not only have roles within the relationship, but responsibilities, as well. If the young person does not have some way to be accountably involved in the relationship, then it is not an "alliance."

The second of the Five Skills is:

The ability to establish therapeutic alliances with young people in which they feel safe, are able to trust, and have a role to play; to use the therapeutic alliance to create resilience-fostering environments; and to recognize that we represent a time-limited part of a young person's environment and childhood experiences. Through the therapeutic alliance, we intentionally utilize every moment of our limited time creating environments and experiences that serve to reduce and heal trauma and foster resilience, within the confines of and in fidelity with *what* we are doing (our job duties and the outcomes we are seeking).

THREE OF FIVE
'Tain't What You Sing (It's the Way That You Sing It)

This is the final piece of advice that Sy and Trummy gave us (after the *way*, *time*, *place*, *bring*, and *swing* it), and we're not really talking about singing. But singing is one form of communication, and communication, particularly communication across cultures, is a far more important skill than many realize, as well as the prerequisite for most if not all of what we're trying to do. It doesn't matter how skilled we may be at teaching, supervision, counseling, therapy, crisis intervention, case management, or resource development; if we can't effectively communicate those skills, we may as well not have them.

Communication is nothing more than sending verbal and physical cues, which are then interpreted by the receiver, who will then send verbal and physical cues in response. Good communication occurs when those verbal and physical cues are interpreted as intended; but this is by no means a guarantee. There are many factors that contribute to how we interpret things, not the least of which is culture, which is why, when working with people from different cultures, we need to understand their frame of reference and how they interpret our verbal and physical cues in order to successfully communicate with them. An example of how culture can impact meaning was demonstrated when George Bush (the elder) visited Australia and gave the "V" for Victory sign to a crowd. Unfortunately, he did so with his palm facing toward him instead of facing out, which in the Australian culture is no different from the middle finger in American culture. His attempt to communicate one message communicated quite a different message, indeed.

The greatest challenge to cross-cultural work is *communication*, and almost every issue arising from well-intentioned work with other cultures is an issue of *miscommunication*. What does this have to do with working with young people? The simple fact is that, even if a young person and an adult ostensibly share a common culture, it is still an inter-cultural relationship, as youth is a culture of its own. And most issues arising from well-intentioned work with young people are issues of *mis-*(or *poor*)-*communication*.

Youth as a culture

Culture can be defined as the collective attitudes, mores, and behavioral characteristics of a specific social group; a *social group* being two or more people who regularly interact and share a sense of unity and common identity. In a way, we are always working cross-culturally whenever we interact with another human being, as no one exists within a single culture. We have racial cultures, ethnic cultures, national cultures, regional cultures, local cultures, family cultures, work and organizational cultures, and a host of others. Each of these cultures has defined attitudes, mores, and behavioral expectations that create unique frames of reference and impact the member's interpretation of verbal and physical communication cues.

We also have age cultures, with the clearest example being *youth* culture, which results from two primary influences. First, young people are a *segregated* group that exists outside of adult culture. Generally speaking, adults work and raise families, have economic and political power, and enjoy rights and privileges not available to young people; while young people are in the care of parents, caretakers and/or educational systems, and are denied many of the rights and responsibilities of adults. This influence alone creates a different relationship to the world and, in turn, results in uncommon frames of reference with adults.

Second, young people have a different relationship to *time*, if for no other reason than their age. For a 10-year-old a year is one tenth of their life and feels like an interminable length of time; whereas for a 40-year-old, that same span of time is only one fortieth of their life and seems to pass much more quickly[2]. Everything we do, including our communication, is impacted by how we perceive time. For example, a young student may ask "What about X?" A teacher may reply; "We'll be discussing X soon." In the teacher's mind, "soon" may mean next week, whereas the student may spend the rest of the lesson waiting for "soon," and then may feel ignored or put off when "soon," in the student's perception, never comes.

Communication traits of adult culture

Much of adult communication is based on implication (a conclusion drawn from that which is not explicitly stated) and assumed knowledge (a statement based on the presupposition that the listener already has knowledge of information supporting the statement). Adults also tend to speak in metaphors, as these lend themselves to both implication and assumed knowledge. If you suggest a course of action and the response you get is … "That's a slippery slope that might end up biting you in the butt" … you know exactly what is being said to you; even though you're not on any slope, slippery or otherwise, and nothing is actually going to bite any part of your body. As a thought experiment one day, pay attention to all of the communication you send or receive, verbally or otherwise; you may be surprised by how much of it contains one or more metaphor. But the younger a person is, the more likely they are to be unfamiliar with metaphors, and they may have no idea what you're talking about. This doesn't mean that metaphors will always be beyond a youth's comprehension, but where communication may be a challenge, avoiding metaphor reduces the risk of a miscommunication.

Communication traits of youth culture

Young people communicate much differently than do adults. One of the most distinguishing characteristics of youth

---

[2] This is described in greater detail in my book Street Culture 2.0, An Epistemology of Street-dependent Youth.

communication is that it tends toward the *literal*. Young people do not have the history or experience with communicating ideas as do adults, if for no other reason than they haven't been doing it as long. This is particularly true of very young children, but it can be seen even in the communication style of older adolescents. In fact, communication is one of the traits affected by trauma and delayed development, and a child who has experienced either will tend to communicate at a much "younger" level than their chronological age. This creates inter-cultural communication issues when an adult assumes that a young person is able to extrapolate the meaning of what is being said to them, as well as when an adult assumes additional meaning of a youth's statement beyond its literal meaning.

How words are interpreted is another pitfall of youth/adult communication. It is by no means certain that a young person will assign the same meaning to the words you use as you intend, or that you will interpret the meaning of a word used by a young person in the way they intended. Why? Because, particularly in the English language, words have multiple meanings … and not simply a few meanings, but sometimes hundreds. NPR reported 645 definitions for the word "run," and one online dictionary site claims that the top ten multiple definition words in the English language have between them 3,264 different meanings … that's an average of 326.4 definitions per word. Another list of the 500 most commonly used words in the English language reports 14,000 different definitions for those words, bringing the average down to "only" 28 meanings per word. When this is taken into consideration, it becomes less surprising that we sometimes fail to communicate, and a bit of a miracle that we are able to communicate at all.

And these interpretation issues don't even take into account a communication pitfall known as "Culturally-loaded Vocabulary." This includes words that don't actually exist outside of a specified culture, and words that do exist but have a definition within a culture that may not have made it into the dictionary yet. The end result is that it is more common than one might think to have youth/adult communication where both parties recognize the words but assign radically different meanings to those words. If you've ever been involved in an easy conversation with a young person that suddenly and inexplicably just seems to go off the rails, you've experienced the impact of recognizing the words being used, but not attaching the same meaning to those words.

A third communication pitfall is a young person's concept of time, which is much more present-oriented than that of an adult. Again, adults tend to extrapolate and plan forward, whereas young people tend to reflect in the moment. If a young person tells you something about how they think or feel, it is a mistake to take that information as set in stone (See? Adults use metaphors a lot!). Instead, it should be interpreted as a reflection of how they are thinking and feeling *right now*, which may or may not reflect what they think or feel *generally*.

Communication responsibility

In a therapeutic alliance between an adult helper (e.g., teacher, probation officer, outreach worker) and a youth client (e.g., student, juvenile offender, street-dependent youth), the responsibility for bridging the cultural communication gap lies with the adult. We have to recognize our communication bias and adapt to a young person's communication style. Why? Well, let's leave aside for a moment the fact that we are professionals working with clients and it is incumbent upon us to do so effectively. Let's instead focus on the fact that in any youth/adult relationship, the adult will have more power in that relationship. As the more powerful person in the relationship, adults have the greater influence on the nature of the relationship, and therefore have the responsibility to ensure that the less powerful benefits from the relationship. This does not mean that we need to "talk like the kids" . . . in fact, attempting to do so will come across as phony, no matter how good you are at it. What it does mean is that we need to comprehend how young people communicate in order to understand, and to be understood.

Youth/adult communication techniques

Here are 4 things to be aware of when communicating with young people in order to fulfill our responsibility to understand, and to be understood:

1. Speak and listen literally

Do not assume meaning on the part of young people. Listen to
what they are actually saying and focus on what their words literally
mean. When speaking, avoid euphemism, metaphor, idiom, or
anything else that relies on insinuation or assumed knowledge, unless
you are certain that the young person will understand your intent.
Communicate what you wish to say directly, and with as little room
for misunderstanding as possible.

2. Pay attention to interpretation

Remember, words have multiple meanings, and different cultures
sometimes assign meanings to words that we may not share. Pay less
attention to the words being used, and greater attention to *how* the
words are being used. If you have any doubt, assume that you don't
understand, and ask for clarification. When speaking, avoid $16
words and use simple language. This is not because young people are
incapable, it's simply because they are less experienced with language
than are adults. It also helps to reduce misinterpretation, as simpler
words are less likely to confuse. If you hear yourself say something
that might be misunderstood, pause and clarify. Don't ask if the
young person knows what you mean, as saying "yes" only means that
they either *think* they know what you mean or are embarrassed to
admit that they don't. Instead, pause and say something like ... "what
I mean by that is;" and then restate it in a more direct manner.
Likewise, when a youth uses a term that may have different
meanings, say something like; "When I use that word, I mean ... is
that what you mean?" You may be surprised by how often the
answer is "no."

3. Remain present-oriented

Speak and think in terms of the present. Even if a young person
is talking about the past or the future, they are reflecting on it from a
present-oriented perspective. A useful technique in overcoming
present conflicts is to let a few minutes go by and return to the topic
using past tense language. For example, if a youth is angry about
something, take a break, or get a glass of water, or find some other

way to pause for a few minutes; then return to the topic using language that puts the event into the past. Don't say "why are you angry," or "are you still angry," but instead say something like "why *were* you so angry?" The more you can verbally place the event in the past, the less "connected" to the event the young person will feel and the easier it will be for them to examine their feelings objectively.

Of course, it is our job to help them transition from a present-oriented perspective and learn to plan for the future; to connect current activity with future results. But this is a process, not a destination, and all you can do is influence the process … you are unlikely to fully achieve the goal; if for no other reason than future planning is an executive function of the brain, and a young person's prefrontal cortex, responsible for executive functions, is not yet fully developed. For this reason, the best way to work on future orientation issues is to do so in the short term. Don't focus too much on how what they do today may affect them in 5 or 10 years. Instead, make connections between their choices and behavior today and how it may affect them in a few days. The more we connect present choices with short term future results, the more likely it we will be to help them develop the ability to make longer term connections.

4. Balance power

With few exceptions, in almost every circumstance involving an adult and a young person, the adult has greater power. The dynamics of youth/adult power imbalance will be covered in the examination of the next skill (Respond, don't React), but for our purpose here it is only necessary to accept that adults, generally speaking, have greater power than young people; particularly in relationships of a professional nature. That means that, as adults, we will always be communicating *from* a position of power, and the young people we serve will always be communicating *to* a position of power.

When we speak of power in this context, we are speaking of the ability to do or act in a particular way, and/or the ability to direct or influence events or the behavior of others. We could also be speaking of the ability to use coercion or force, and too many young people are exposed to coercion or force in the form of abuse or neglect, even within systems designed to be helpful and supportive. But, assuming that you are reading this because you are a competent youth worker who does not abuse children, it is still important to be aware of the power we have and how that impacts youth in our care, as well as the power that young people lack, and how that influences their communication with us.

To understand how a power imbalance impacts communication, one only needs to consider the synonyms and antonyms for the word *power*. Roget's 21st Century Thesaurus, Third Edition, lists words that mean exactly or nearly the same as power as *capability, capacity, function, influence, potential, skill, talent, aptitude, competency, dynamism, effectiveness, efficacy, endowment, faculty, gifts, potentiality,* and *qualification*. These are all terms that speak to one's competence and authority. Now consider the words listed as opposite in meaning; *impotence, inability, incapacity, incompetence, lack, weakness, failure, inaptitude, loss, uselessness, debility, disability, impairment, infirmity, subservience, surrender,* and *yielding*. Notice the difference? Can you see how communication might be affected if one person is characterized by the first list, and the other is characterized by the second?

When I directed programs I had to be conscious of power imbalance even when speaking with my staff. Since I was their supervisor, with the power and authority to hold them accountable and even terminate their employment, I clearly held greater power in the relationship. If I truly wanted their input and to know their thoughts on matters, I had to hold back on expressing my own … because the minute "The Boss" spoke it would affect how they responded. The same is true in any unequal power relationship. If we do not consciously work to mitigate the imbalance of power, then our attempts to communicate will more often than not become little more than lectures.

The first, and most important, step towards mitigating the power imbalance in youth/adult communication is to simply be aware of it, understand how it impacts communication, and consciously desire to address it. If we can do that, we will notice when a power imbalance is affecting communication and see opportunities to reduce its impact. But here are a few simple things we can do that will help:

a) Adults are often *physically* more powerful. Particularly with early to pre-adolescent young people, adults tend to be taller, larger, and more physically matured. Be aware of your body language. Maintain "open" stances and avoid positioning yourself where your physical presence may be intimidating. Sit or squat rather than talking "down" (physically) to a youth.

b) Be aware of "power positions," such as sitting behind a desk or in a room's dominant position. Avoid, or even allow the young person to occupy, the power position.

c) Be aware of the power of touch. Note that it is always the person in a more powerful position who *initiates* touch. A member of your School Board or Board of Directors may place a supportive hand on an employee's shoulder or pat them on the back; but an employee does not walk into a Board meeting and do the same. Avoid initiating unnecessary touch, and always ask permission before initiating any kind of touch. The one exception to this would be in situations where restraint is required. It should go without saying that restraint should always be a last resort and least preferable option, but when it is used, it should be done without malice and with explanation. Asking permission is not appropriate in these situations, but calmly explaining what you're doing while you're doing it can often help to de-escalate, or at least avoid further escalation.

d) Avoid "power plays" that deliberately highlight the power differential. Threats, warnings, and assertions of authority are clearly in this category, but so are less obvious things like asking questions to which you already know the answer. Questions like that are simply power plays in the form of traps. Instead of asking "did you break the window" when you already know that they did, ask "why (or how) did you break the window?"

e) Remember that people, particularly young people, have limited cognitive capacity. Cognitive psychologist George A. Miller first proposed this in a 1956 article published in Psychology Review titled The Magical Number Seven, Plus or Minus Two: Some Limits on Our Capacity for Processing Information. The idea is that the human brain can only cognitively deal with about seven, plus or minus two (7+/-2, or a minimum of five, and up to nine) "chunks" of information at a time. This is important to communication in two ways.

First, it impacts the amount of information that a youth can deal with at any one time, and if we exceed that amount, the youth will either shut down or become overwhelmed ... in any case, we will not get the response and follow-through for which we are hoping. We also need to be aware of the multiplicity of our expectations. For example, if we ask a young person to keep an appointment in the morning, that may sound like one thing to us. But to the young person it may involve figuring out how to wake up on time, what clothes to wear, where to catch the bus, what times the bus runs and what time they need to catch it in order to make the appointment, how to deal with fares and transfers, how to get to the appointment from where the bus drops them off, and the entire bus process in reverse in order to get home again. Depending on a youth's knowledge and experience, a simple request to keep an appointment may already be pushing the upper limits of or exceeding a young person's cognitive capacity.

The second way it affects communication is directly responsible for all those times we've exasperatingly expressed sentiments like "I very clearly said ...," or "It's like they're just not listening!" This is the result one of two pitfalls (or both). Either we've overcommunicated (we spoke in paragraphs instead of sentences, or words), resulting in more than 7+/-2 "chunks" of information in our statement, question, or direction; or we haven't communicated often enough. The 7+/-2 theory also correlates with the number of times new information needs to be communicated before it begins to "sink in." We should expect that if we want a young person to know or to do something, we're going to have to communicate it to them at least 5 times, maybe as many as 9 or more, before they "get it" (and it helps if we use different means of communication to address all learning styles).

A good rule of thumb with application of the 7+/-2 rule is; when communicating information or knowledge, err on the high side (9 or more), and when requiring action or follow-through, err on the low side (5 or less things to do at a time).

Finally, if the goal is communication, then we are talking about an exchange of ideas. The best way to ensure that happens is to . . . well . . . shut up and listen. If you have spoken for more than, say, two or three sentences, you are no longer communicating; you're lecturing, and lecturing young people is the surest way for them to stop listening to you.

The third of the Five Skills is:

The ability to communicate cross-culturally with young people, paying attention to the impact of literalness, word interpretation, present-orientation, and power imbalance. It is the consistent focus on understanding and being understood, tempered with the awareness that young people communicate differently than adults, that is the foundation for this skill.

FOUR OF FIVE
Respond, Don't React

All work with young people, regardless of the milieu in which it takes place, or the approach being utilized, is little more than a series of reciprocal actions. The words, actions, and behavior of each member in a therapeutic alliance influences the words, actions and behavior of the other. While the contributions to child development and psychology of people like Ainsworth, Erikson, and Piaget are well known, one of the most important and often ignored contributions came from a 17th century mathematician, astronomer, and physicist by the name of Sir Isaac Newton.

Physics meets youth work

In 1687, Newton first published what has become known as Newton's Laws of Motion. They consist of three "laws" that describe the relationship between bodies and the forces that act upon them and, together, these three laws became the foundation for classical mechanics. It is the third of Newton's laws of which those who work with young people need to be aware . . . though, in fairness, it is pertinent to youth work in an analogous sense.

Newton's Third Law of Motion has been stated in many different ways in the 300+ years since it was first proposed, but in its most common form it is simply; *for every action, there is an equal and opposite reaction.* In other words, objects act upon each other, and if you push something, it pushes back with equal force.

Youth work is analogous to this law in that every therapeutic alliance consists of a series of actions and reactions. The adult professional acts toward the youth client in a certain way, and the youth client reacts to that action. In the same way, the youth client acts toward the adult professional, and the adult professional will react to that action. This sets up a relationship where an adult professional and a youth client are in an on-going dance of actions and reactions ... or, more accurately, an initial action, followed by a series of mutual reactions.

Action, reaction, and power

This pattern works well in an equal-power relationship where each party has equal ability to influence and be influenced by the other. But in adult/youth relationships of unequal power, such as those between parent and child, or teacher and student, or probation officer and offender, or outreach worker and street-dependent youth, the power imbalance changes the equation. The person with greater power in the relationship (the adult) has greater freedom to act and influence, and the person with lesser power in the relationship (the young person) has lesser influence and carries greater risk. In an equal-power relationship, if I react with anger my greatest risk is that I may upset or hurt the feelings of the other person. In an unequal power relationship, the less powerful person is at an extreme disadvantage. If I react with anger to my teacher, or my probation officer, or my outreach worker, it may affect my grade, or my freedom, or the resources available to me.

Conversely, the more powerful person may react without consequence. They may express anger, or frustration, they may react with sarcasm or ridicule, or they may express fear or even hostility, and they may be free from direct personal consequences. In some cases, such as if they directly violate policies or professional expectations, there may be some consequences for their reactions, but more often than not, negative reactions are brief and go unwitnessed, and the only real consequence of their reaction is suffered by their less powerful target; possibly in the loss of privileges or services, and definitely in the loss of positive benefit from the relationship. There can also be additional self-inflicted consequences, as the less powerful may internalize the more powerful's reaction, concluding that they deserve such treatment because they are bad, inadequate, or simply unworthy.

Changing the equation

Admittedly, negative reactions as extreme as I'm describing are fortunately the exception in youth work, not the rule. While abuse does happen in our field, such abuse is not supported by the field, and where it occurs, it is hopefully identified and dealt with either by removing the offending adult from service, or providing the training needed to eliminate that worker's deficits. But it is not the big, obvious behaviors with which we as individuals need be concerned … it is our struggle with our own human reactions to the behaviors, challenges, and moral conflicts that we face daily in youth work. We are human beings with human failings in positions of power over vulnerable young people, and that reality means that we don't have the luxury of being the sole recipient of the consequences of our reactions, as the young person to whom we react will always experience some of those consequences.

There's only one way to protect the youth in our care from the consequences of our human reactions, and it's not at all easy. It is, however, the mark of a true youth work professional. We have to train ourselves to break the Newtonian action/reaction cycle and take our reactions out of the equation, replacing action/reaction with action/*response*. The goal is to be able to professionally *respond* regardless of how we may emotionally *react*.

Reacting versus responding

Etymology may help us to understand the difference between reacting and responding. The word "react" is originally derived from the Latin "reagere," with "re" meaning "back" and "agere" meaning "to do, perform." In other words, literally to "go back" to a "previous performance." In the 1600's it evolved to "react," literally to "re-act," or to "perform again." When we react to something, we are "re-performing" how that thing affects *us*. It is not about the outside stimuli itself, it is about how that outside stimuli affects us *personally*, and that may be very different for different people. Some people, depending on their life experience, personal mores, and musical taste, react to rap music extremely positively, while others may have profound negative reactions to the exact same stimuli, but viewed through the lens of different life experience, personal mores, and musical taste. Again, a reaction is all about the one reacting and meets their *personal* needs in dealing with the stimuli.

Respond also has Latin roots, utilizing the same "re" (back) combined with "pondere," meaning "to pledge." In the 1300's the French adopted this term wholly, and evolved the meaning to "correspond, answer to, promise in return." In other words, to respond is to answer and communicate to the outside stimuli. It is about *the other*, and what needs to be *given in return*.

In a therapeutic youth work alliance, which is more important and offers the greatest benefit for the young person in our care; to *react* to our personal needs, or to *respond* to theirs? For any competent youth worker, the question is rhetorical. Whether we are paid or volunteering, it is our job to respond to the young person's needs. The only reason why the young person is in our care in the first place is to receive assistance from us. Reacting rather than responding is not only potentially harmful to the young person, it is a dereliction of duty. That doesn't mean that our reactions and personal needs are unimportant … indeed, our own personal growth and mental health depends on examining and understanding our reactions and meeting our personal needs … but that's what supervisors, close personal relationships, and therapists are for. It is never appropriate to *react* to the young people in our care, what is always required is a professional *response*.

Now for some bad news. Even if we understand and support the concept that we need to *respond* rather than *react*, doing so is extremely challenging and requires a high degree of self-awareness and reflection. *How* and *when* we react also depends a great deal on the stimuli to which we are reacting. Different stimuli will trigger different forms of reaction in us, and these different reactions become progressively harder to recognize and control. Primarily there are three different "levels" of reaction that human beings experience; Investigatory, Pavlovian, and Inborn.

1. Investigatory Reactions

This first "level" of reaction is the easiest to recognize and replace with a professional response. It occurs at the conscious level and is triggered by stimuli where we want to know more or further explore a stimulus. In many cases it's not a bad thing, as there are often situations where wanting to know more or explore further is therapeutically called for, but, even in such circumstances, knowing more or exploring further should be done out of a professional response rather than an investigatory reaction. Why? Because there are also circumstances where wanting to know more or explore further is not therapeutically called for at all and may present risks for the young person. Having our curiosity triggered is not in and of itself suggestive of a therapeutic need of the young person.

Recognizing an investigatory reaction in ourselves is critical to asking an important question before proceeding, and that question is; *why do I need to know about or further understand this?* If we can't answer that question with something that directly identifies a therapeutic need of the young person, then our wanting to know more or explore is meeting *our* needs, not theirs. And if we can answer it with a reason that benefits the young person, then we still should professionally respond rather than proceed on our investigatory reaction, as any knowledge seeking or further investigation with a young person may lead to vulnerabilities, experiences, and/or traumas for which we need to be prepared. Following our curiosity in response to stimulus from the young people in our care is analogous to skipping through a minefield, with equally analogous consequences for both us and our clients.

2. Pavlovian Reactions

Ivan Petrovich Pavlov was a Russian physiologist best known for his work in classical conditioning. By pairing food with the ringing of a bell, Pavlov discovered that he could trigger an innate response ... salivation, which dogs do in response to food ... by simply ringing a bell. In other words, something natural to the dogs could be triggered by conditioning the dogs to associate their natural response with something else. This became known as Pavlovian Conditioning.

Years later an American psychologist named John Broadus Watson applied Pavlov's research to human beings, beginning with an 11-month old infant. He presented a white rat to the child, who initially showed no fear whatsoever of the rodent. He then began presenting the rat to the non-fearful child, but paired the experience with a loud, jarring noise that scared the infant. The child then developed a fear of the rat, regardless of whether the noise was present. Watson's ethically questionable experiment (by today's standards) implied that Pavlov's classical conditioning could create phobias in human beings.

But classical conditioning is not limited to the creation of phobias. Many of the reactions we have to different stimuli are the result of our own classical conditioning. When a song comes on the radio and suddenly our spirits lift due to our positive associations with that song, we are experiencing a Pavlovian reaction from our classical conditioning to that song. Similarly, we bring our classical conditioning with us into our youth work profession, and experience classical conditioning *by* our youth work experience, that creates Pavlovian reactions that may not be consistent with the professional response that would best serve the young person in our care.

Pavlovian reactions occur at the line between our conscious and subconscious awareness, and as such are more difficult to recognize than are investigatory reactions, but we can still train ourselves to recognize when a Pavlovian reaction is triggered. The triggers are often challenges to our beliefs, mores, or preferences, and the tell-tale signs may be physical, emotional, or judgmental reactions that are not justified by the stimulus. For example, a young person asks us for something and we immediately react as though we are being manipulated or lied to.

That may be, but we simply don't have enough information yet to make that determination. Instead, we are having a Pavlovian reaction based on our classical conditioning by other young people in similar situations. To be as effective as we can be in this moment, we need to recognize our Pavlovian reaction, suppress that reaction, and proceed with a professional response to the young person's request.

Other signals of Pavlovian reactions may include physical signs, such as tensing up, or emotional reactions, such as irritability or disgust. We all have different signs of Pavlovian reactions based on our own personalities and experiences; just as we will all react differently to similar forms of stimuli. The exact same action by a young person may create a Pavlovian reaction in one teacher or staff, but not another (which explains why some teacher/staff seem to be able to work with a youth that other teacher/staff can't; it's not about the young person, it's about teacher/staff's *reaction* to that young person). This is not about understanding young people, this is about understanding ourselves, and, as we say in our field, understanding our "buttons;" the things that trigger reactions in us. It is about being self-aware enough to recognize when we are having Pavlovian reactions and replacing them with professional responses.

3. Inborn Reactions

While we are fully or partially conscious of our investigatory and Pavlovian reactions, this third category presents our greatest challenge due to it being instinctive, that is, it is an innate, natural reaction that we possess from birth. It is automatic and unlearned, and therefore not something over which we exert a great deal of conscious control. While many of our emotions tend to be more cognitive, such as guilt or jealousy, inborn reactions involve emotions and physiological reactions believed to be more biological than cognitive. These are our "base" emotions and physiologies such as fear, anger, hunger, pleasure, pain, frustration, etc. When these base reactions are triggered, we immediately provide context for them. For example, we're walking in a city and suddenly we feel fearful. In order to address our fear, we need to know what we are fearful of, and we will quickly create a context that justifies our fear. In some cases, the context is easy and correct … if there's an active shooter on the street, our fear has an obvious and accurate source. But in many cases base emotions will surface in situations where the context is not readily apparent, and we will *create* a context based on our perception of the situation, and our knowledge and life experience up to that point.

The context we create determines the reaction we demonstrate. For example, we're in a grocery store and we see a disheveled adolescent stealing and eating some food without paying for it, triggering an inborn response of anger. As soon as our anger is aroused, we provide context. Maybe our context is that he's a lazy slacker who doesn't give a crap about property rights or the cost of his action on others, and our anger motivates us to possibly intervene, or at least report the teen to the authorities. But what if, due to our personal knowledge and life experience, we apply a different context? What if we see the teen as a homeless youth who hasn't had a meal in days? In that case our anger might be directed at the teen's *circumstances*, and we either let the teen get away with it, or perhaps even reach out to buy the teen a meal.

While we have little or no control over our inborn reactions, the context we create is a form of Pavlovian reaction, and that puts it back into a level of consciousness. Once there, we do have some control … at least enough to recognize that we are emotionally *reacting*, which gives us the opportunity to replace our emotional reaction with a professional *response*.

What does it mean to professionally respond?

Reactions do not require any volition; that is, they are not willful. There is no intention or deliberation involved in a reaction. A response, however, is a thoughtful, deliberate action intended to communicate a specific message in pursuit of a desirable outcome. To professionally respond means to recognize and set aside our personal needs, desires, beliefs, perceptions, comfort … all of our personal reactions to the stimuli ... and understand the young person's behavior in the context of what *they* need in that moment, then *respond* to that young person's need. Do not misunderstand this as meaning that you should always give the young person what they want or are asking for; it means to focus on the psycho-emotional and/or physical needs of the young person, and provide a *therapeutic* response; that is, a response intended to heal or relieve a disorder.

4 steps toward a professional response

Step One: Recognize our reactions

How do we know when we are reacting? What are our personal signs? Is it feeling offended? Is it feeling protectiveness or concern? Does our stomach tense up? Does our mouth feel dry? There are likely a variety of signals that we are reacting to something, and those signals may be different to different stimuli, but the key is to become adequately self-aware to be able to notice when something is affecting us on a personal level. The first step toward replacing reactions with responses is to recognize when we are reacting.

Step Two: Interrupt our reactions

It is said so often that we sometimes miss it, but we can't help others until we help ourselves. Every time we fly, we sit through the same safety announcement that tells us that, in the event of a loss of cabin pressure, oxygen masks will fall from the ceiling. Should that happen, and should we be sitting with someone who needs assistance, we should put our *own* mask on *first*. A person requiring assistance does not benefit from a mask if all the people who can provide assistance have passed out.

The efficacy of our assistance is compromised if we are reacting, and we may even cause harm. Once we recognize that we are reacting, we have to *stop* before we can proceed. In cases where we have the luxury of time, that may mean taking a break, getting a glass of water, or just letting something go for now. In cases that are more immediate or crisis oriented, it may mean just taking a deep breath, or finding some other way to interrupt our reaction. A helpful method of reaction interruption is to create a "reaction talisman." Usually thought of as an object such as a ring or stone, a talisman is something that is believed to bring luck or have magical powers. A "reaction talisman" is a grounding object or action that we imbue with the power to interrupt our reactions. It serves as both a reminder and as something to do when we are aware that we are reacting. In my personal experience, I rely on an object *and* an action to serve as my reaction talisman. My object is a small Hematite crystal carried in my pocket. When reacting, I can touch the crystal or, more often, simply focus on its weight in my pocket to interrupt my reaction. In more serious and immediate cases, I used an action; pinching the web-like area between my thumb and index finger with the thumb and index finger of my other hand; giving me a reaction talisman at the ready in every situation.

Note that the goal here is not to stop our reaction ... we may not be able to do that. The goal is to *interrupt* our reaction and *set it aside for now*, clearing the way for a professional response.

Step Three: Identify the disorder

A professional response is treatment, that is, it is intended to heal or relieve a disorder. To do that, we have to be able to properly diagnose the disorder that is in immediate need of treatment. Rarely will the disorder be the source of our reactions. In most cases, we are reacting to the young person's reaction to the disorder. Maybe a young person is all up in our face cursing at us. We are reacting with fear of their proximity and aggressiveness, along with anger at their disrespect, and shock at their offensive use of language. But none of that is the disorder in need of treatment. In most cases such as this the young person is reacting to strong emotions that are beyond their capacity to control and, regardless of any other needs, the *immediate* need is to regain emotional control. The professional response called for has nothing to do with their behavior or the cause of their behavior; what is needed is a response that helps them to re-establish emotional control. Until and unless the young person is able to re-establish emotional control, no other form of intervention is likely to have any positive effect.

Step Four: Treat the disorder

A professional response provides treatment for the identified disorder. In the case of a loss of emotional control, the treatment required is de-escalation directed at helping the young person regain control. It is not the time to take offense at their language, or question their reaction, or reason with them about their behavior, as your own reactions may be telling you to do. The disorder requiring treatment is a loss of emotional control, and the professional response required is one that de-escalates the emotional intensity in order to help the young person regain control.

To respond rather than react; be prepared

Plans for dealing with any crisis always focus on preparation. We conduct fire drills, Active Shooter drills, and stock emergency supplies for earthquakes and other natural disasters for one simple reason; should such a crisis occur there will be no time to learn how or prepare to respond. To be in a position to survive the crisis, we must have done our thinking about and preparation for the crisis *in advance*.

Youth work is no different. When we find ourselves in a difficult situation requiring a response, we may be challenged if that's the first time we've thought about how to respond. This is particularly true if the situation is outside of the normal scope of our work. Some examples; a young person approaches us sexually; or confides in us about criminal behavior; or reveals that they saw us on our off time drinking at a bar. Any one of these possible scenarios, along with many others, could crop up at any time when working with young people. We are also subject to misinterpretations by young people and may find ourselves being accused of things we never intended. For example, while helping a young woman pick out clothes, a worker turned around not realizing that the youth had bent over to pick up a hanger she had dropped, accidentally brushing her butt with his hand. The young woman reacted to that as a sexual assault. You will react in that situation. The question is, how should you professionally respond?

Thinking through situations in advance will better prepare you to professionally respond should such situations occur. A good exercise is to think of worst-case, nightmare scenarios ... the situations we hope we *never* encounter ... and consider how we'll respond should they occur. Such "thought exercises" strengthen our response "muscles" and provide defense against surrendering to emotional reactions.

Our default response setting

No matter how well we prepare, however, there will be times when a professional response is needed, but all we have is an emotional reaction. We may be trained well enough to recognize that a professional response is needed, but at the moment, we got nothin'. In such situations, until we are able to come up with a better response, the best thing to do is to fall back on what should be our "default" response setting; *empathy*.

An empathic response is simply a brief statement that demonstrates that you have heard and understand the other person's concerns or feelings. It is not agreeing with, justifying, or condoning those concerns or feelings, it is simply acknowledging them. It is not summarizing or paraphrasing, which focus on the *content* of what a person is saying. An empathic response reflects the person's *feelings*, not the content of their communication.

Here's an example of the difference between responding to *content* versus responding to *feelings*:

- Young person: I don't like homework. I like to do what I want after school.
- Content response: You think homework takes up too much of your free time.
- Empathic (feelings) response: It can be frustrating having to choose between homework and fun.

39

Note that the content response may trigger the young person into a defense of their position, whereas the feelings response will likely create a sense of being understood.

When we make a mistake

Note that I didn't say *if* we make a mistake. We are human, we are going to react, and sometimes we won't catch it until after we have the reaction. That's OK; in fact, how we respond after we make mistakes can be incredible teaching moments for the young people in our care. The thing to do in such situations is to simply be honest and accept responsibility. We own our reactions, admit to them, and apologize before moving on. The only thing more therapeutically called for than a professional response is accepting responsibility for our reactions when they surface.

The fourth of the Five Skills is:

The ability to recognize our reactions, interrupt them, and replace them with professional responses. It includes accepting responsibility and apologizing when we fail to do so. If we are unsure of what type of professional response is called for, we default to empathy.

FIVE OF FIVE
Embrace Failure

This is arguably the most difficult of the 5 skills, and one which may seem counter-intuitive. Regardless of the context in which we are working with young people, our goal is to help them overcome challenges in their lives and achieve success. This is true whether we are a professional, a volunteer, or even a parent; the challenge we have with the young people in our care is to ensure that they leave our care better prepared to overcome the challenges that face them than they were when they entered our care. But, if that's success for *us*, we make it very difficult to achieve our success if we focus our attention on young people achieving theirs.

"Failures are fingerposts on the road to achievement"

I didn't say that, British novelist C. S. Lewis did ... which is probably why he called them "fingerposts," a traditional type of sign post used primarily in the United Kingdom and the Republic of Ireland. They are signs along roads that point in the direction of travel to specific places. In other words, achievement or "success" may be where you wish to end up, but you are unlikely to get there without the assistance of failure. This is a universal truth that often gets lost or underplayed in youth work. We want so desperately for our young people to be successful (and often we need to document what funders pre-determine to be "success") that we may intentionally avoid or reduce the opportunity for failure; but failure is a necessary ingredient in all success. Think of a balcony at the top of a staircase. The balcony is the success we seek; the stairs are the failures we must overcome to reach it. We will never reach the balcony (success) unless we are willing to experience the stairs (failure).

"Failure is something we can avoid only by saying nothing, doing nothing, and being nothing"

Again, not me. This quote is from Denis Waitley, and it deserves our attention because the youth work field tends to be both focused on success, and failure avoidant; not just in action, but in narrative. From the very beginning of young people's lives they are taught through grading that success is good, and failure is bad. But failure is not bad, it is an unavoidable prerequisite to success, and maintaining success requires embracing failure. Consider this quote from a basketball player you may have heard of; "I've missed more than 9,000 shots in my career. I've lost almost 300 games. 26 times, I've been trusted to take the game winning shot and missed. I've failed over and over and over again in my life." But don't feel sorry for him. His name is Michael Jordan, and the final line of his quote is "And that is why I succeed." He may have missed over 9,000 shots, but he would have missed every shot he didn't take out of a fear of failure.

And Jordan is the rule, not the exception. He is in the company of such famous failures as Oprah Winfrey, who was fired from her first television job; Steven Spielberg, who was twice rejected by the University of Southern California's School of Cinematic Arts; Walt Disney, who was told by one of his early employers that he 'lacked imagination and had no good ideas;' Albert Einstein, who didn't start speaking until he was four, reading until he was seven, and was thought to be mentally handicapped; Theodor Seuss Geisel, AKA Dr Seuss, whose first book was rejected by 27 different publishers; J.K. Rowling, who was a broke, depressed, divorced single mother on welfare before she started writing about a character named Harry Potter; and many others ... likely including yourself. As Rowling once said; "It is impossible to live without failing at something, unless you live so cautiously that you might as well not have lived at all -- in which case, you fail by default."

Reframing failure

How we think about failure can have a direct relationship on how well we prepare young people for success. Traditionally, failure is regarded as the dictionary defines it; *an omission of occurrence or performance; a lack of success.* Note the predominant qualifiers in this definition; "omission" (something neglected or left undone) and "lack" (to be deficient or needing). These are things that we regard negatively; actions and circumstances to be avoided. But if our goal is to help young people succeed, failure *cannot* be avoided; it must be embraced. A huge part of our task in helping young people succeed is to help them learn how to fail. Returning to our staircase-to-the-balcony example, do we consider the stairs to be an omission or lack of the balcony, something to be avoided or jumped over, or do we help young people learn how to *use* the stairs to achieve their goal of reaching the balcony? It's the latter, and we are glad the stairs are there, because without the stairs (failure) we can never reach the balcony (success). If we think of failure as an "omission" or "lack" and try to protect young people from experiencing failure, we will be hindering their path to success, not helping it. But if we reframe failure as a necessary step toward success, we help to make their eventual success much more likely.

Two who reframed

Sir James Dyson created the now well-known bagless vacuum cleaner that bears his name. As a result, he had a net worth of 5.3 billion dollars by 2016. But he was not an overnight success. It took him 15 years, and 5,126 failed prototypes before he perfected his bagless vacuum. If he regarded failure as most people do, he might have given up after a few years and several thousand failures. Instead, he's a billionaire.

Or consider Thomas Edison, who I consider to be the master of failure reframing. Edison was 5 months into his attempt to create a nickel-iron battery when he was visited by an associate named Walter S. Mallory. In "Edison: His Life and Inventions," the following encounter is described:

"I found him at a bench about three feet wide and twelve to fifteen feet long, on which there were hundreds of little test cells that had been made up by his corps of chemists and experimenters. He was seated at this bench testing, figuring, and planning. I then learned that he had thus made over nine thousand experiments in trying to devise this new type of storage battery, but had not produced a single thing that promised to solve the question. In view of this immense amount of thought and labor, my sympathy got the better of my judgment, and I said: 'Isn't it a shame that with the tremendous amount of work you have done you haven't been able to get any results?' Edison turned on me like a flash, and with a smile replied: **<u>Results! Why, man, I have gotten a lot of results! I know several thousand things that won't work</u>.** *"* [emphasis mine]

What Mallory regarded as 9,000 failures to achieve success, Edison regarded as 9,000 successful discoveries of what didn't work. What Mallory thought of as wasted time that brought Edison no closer to his goal, Edison regarded as time well spent that brought him 9,000 steps *closer* to his goal. This is an attitude that make failure impossible, because every failure becomes a success in that it eliminates one more thing that doesn't work. It's an attitude that regards every failure as a successful move closer to your goal; it's another step up the staircase to the balcony.

Embracing failure

Embracing failure is really just enabling success, as the two are inseparable. You won't be able to drive your car if you aren't willing to pay for a tank of gas, and you won't be able to achieve success unless you are willing to "pay" by failing. But how is this applicable to youth work?

Regardless of the circumstances of your work with young people, youth are in our care because of some sort of omission or lack in their lives. Student have an omission or lack of knowledge; adjudicated youth have an omission or lack of demonstrated ability to adhere to the law; youth on the streets have an omission or lack of ability to support themselves and meet their basic needs. We don't think of them, or approach them, as failures when they enter our care (though, in the case of adjudicated youth we may see them through the lens of other negative labels). In fact, we *have* to see them as potentially successful, otherwise there'd be little point in trying to help them. But, once in our care, our willingness to accept "failure" on their part often becomes more challenging; because now their "failures" become a reflection on *us*. If they are not being successful in our class or program, we interpret that as meaning that either we are doing something wrong, or there's an "omission or lack" on the young person's part. Particularly in a group where others are being successful, we may conclude that it must be the young person's "omission or lack." In other words, "failure" on the part of a young person in our care is more often than not seen as a lack of progress, something not working, or problematic resistance, rebellion, or lack of effort or desire on the part of the young person. If this is how we think of failure, then all of our responses will be in the context of responding to something unwanted or undesirable. We add to the false narrative that failure is something to be avoided, and in so doing we work *against* the young person's success.

Embracing is not enabling

When you enable something you make it possible, often even probable. A teacher who advances a student who has clearly not learned the lesson is enabling. A probation officer who does not hold a young person accountable to the terms of probation is enabling. A street-outreach worker who makes street survival easier without accompanying efforts to move them off of the streets is enabling. But embracing failure is a very different thing than enabling failure in that enabling *tolerates* failure, whereas embracing *uses* it.

The term "embrace" carries three primary definitions. One refers to a hug, and a second refers to the willingness to accept or support something. It's the third definition that is applicable to embracing failure in youth work; *to include or contain (something) as a constituent part.* Using myself as an example I might say my career embraces a number of activities -- training, consulting, advocacy, and writing. Similarly, when we embrace failure in youth work it's like describing "success" as "a number of activities -- effort, failure, reflection, and growth," which I call the Four Supports to Success. To succeed at anything, one needs to make efforts toward the goal, experience failure in one's efforts, reflect on the experience gained from the failures, and grow from that experience and apply that growth to new efforts; which starts the process all over again until the goal is successfully attained. When we talk about 3 out of 4 of these supports we are unquestionably describing things that are good and desirable. A young person who is making efforts is a *good* thing; a young person reflecting on their experience is a *good* thing; a young person who experiences personal growth from their reflection is a *good* thing. So how can we possible consider the second support, failure, to be a *bad* thing? It isn't, and we shouldn't think of it or expose young people to the belief or attitude that it is.

Of course, the Four Supports may lose their status as "good" things if they are not used together. A young person who makes minimal efforts here and there but never sees them through will not be successful. A young person who experiences failure and gives up will not be successful. A young person who does little more than reflect on life, without ever putting the knowledge gained to use will not be successful. And a young person who hopes for growth without making efforts, failing, and reflecting on their failure will not be successful. But a youth worker who hopes to help a young person be successful by encouraging effort, reflection, and growth, while discouraging and distaining failure, will be far less effective than one who embraces a youth's failures and helps the young person to embrace them as well.

Putting the Four Supports into action

Embracing failure in youth work is as simple (and challenging) as embracing the Four Supports. Let's examine each in turn.

The First Support: Effort

Let's be perfectly clear about one thing right off the bat; we are not talking about *your* effort, we are talking about the young person's. There are two extremely difficult rules that youth workers must follow if they are going to be effective:

Rule #1: Never do anything for a young person that they can and should do for themselves.

This is a very difficult rule for youth workers because we want to help. Sometimes we attempt to "jump start" a young person's efforts by subsidizing them with our efforts, but inevitably what we do is undermine the young person's efforts. Human beings naturally tend to follow the path of least resistance, and if we replace their efforts with ours, the path of least resistance that we create for them is to sit back and let us do the work. This does not mean that we don't help, but it does mean that we understand the difference between "helping" and "doing for." This is where the Youth Development structure of "SOS" (Services, Opportunities, and Supports) comes into play. "Services" are anything we do "to or for" young people. They are sometimes necessary ... a homeless youth may need us *to* provide temporary housing *for* the young person. But "services;" doing "to or for" young people; does not promote growth or lead to success. Services may provide a necessary foundation for growth and success ... a young person who sleeps on the streets will face greater challenges than a young person who has access to safe shelter ... but services are foundational only. To promote growth and success, a young person needs Opportunities (things done *by* a young person acting in or on the world; exploring, expressing, earning, belonging, influencing, and, most importantly, *failing*), and Supports (things done *with* a young person while acting in a secondary or subordinate role; relationships and resources that assist a young person who is pursuing Opportunities). And one of the most important supports an adult can provide for a young person is helping them to anticipate, experience, and grow and learn from the gift of failure. This means that if they *can* do it for themselves, they *should* do it for themselves; even if ... actually, *because* ... they may fail.

Two caveats here. First, we sometimes step in and do *for* because we deem a young person not yet capable of doing something. But not yet being capable is not a reason to do *for* because they will never become capable without effort and failure. Consider our staircase to the balcony example. Suppose your new puppy doesn't know how to climb the stairs. You could "help" the puppy by picking him up and carrying him to the balcony, but I promise you, you'll be doing that when he's a full-grown hound. Or, you could support the puppy while it struggles. Eventually, it will learn to climb the stairs and you'll be relieved from a lifetime of dog-carrying duty. However, if a young person is *incapable* of doing something, we shouldn't expect that they can. For example; a young person may not yet be capable of making phone calls and navigating a system to receive the assistance they need. This may be a reason to do *with*, but it is not a reason to do *for*, because the young person's lack of capability is due to a lack of experience or knowledge. They may "fail" in their first few attempts; like the puppy climbing the steps; but that's good, because through such failure they will learn to succeed. If you make the calls for them, though, they will never develop the capability to make the calls themselves. On the other hand, if a young person is actually *incapable* of doing something we should not expect them to be capable of it. Say they suffer from extreme acrophobia; expecting them to apply for that skyscraper window-washing job should be deferred to a time after they've overcome their acrophobia.

Second, in all cases we are "triaging" a young person's needs. Regardless of what type of youth work we are doing, the young people with whom we work will present a multiplicity of challenges and needs. Sometimes we may need to do "to or for" in response to one need in order to properly address a greater need. For example, maybe a young person has not yet learned the cause and effect of being late for appointments, and they show up an hour late for a scheduled time. In response to this it is often appropriate to reschedule the appointment rather than reinforce the youth's problematic relationship with appointment keeping by seeing them anyway. However, suppose the appointment is for a medical issue they are having that really needs treatment. It may be more important to treat the young person even if late, than it is to help them learn the importance of being on time.

Rule #2: Never work harder than the young person does.

This is another tough one, particularly when working with youth who appear unmotivated. But remember that young people (in fairness, all people) will always seek the path of least resistance. If you are working harder than they are, young people will naturally tend to let you; in which case you will be working on *your* growth, not theirs. Except when needing to provide foundational support (food, clothing, shelter) that a youth cannot currently provide for themselves, we should always be working *with*, not *for*. In my consulting career I have often visited programs where a case manager is knocking him or herself out advocating for a young person who is sitting on the couch watching TV. Even if the advocacy is successful, a young person does not grow and learn from *your* efforts; they grow and learn from *theirs*. It may be the case that we know how to do it and they don't, but they will never know how to do it unless they try (and fail) themselves.

A question I often get in response to Rule #2 is; "OK, then. If I'm not going to work harder than the young person, and the young person is unmotivated, how can I motivate them?" Well, this may be the most frustrating thing that I share with you in this book, because the answer is; *you can't*. Motivation comes from within, not from others. But it's not all bad news. While we may not be able to motivate others, we can create the conditions that inspire others to motivate themselves. But in creating motivational conditions it's important to understand the difference between *motivation* and *manipulation*.

Motivation is the desire or willingness to do something. Note that both desire (a strong feeling of wanting to have something or wishing for something to happen) and willingness (the quality or state of being psychologically prepared to do something; readiness) come from within. I can't make you want or wish for something, nor can I create a state of (psycho-emotional) readiness to do something. These things come from exposure to conditions that create these feelings within, and I *can* create those conditions. However, manipulation (the action of controlling or influencing a person or situation cleverly, unfairly, or unscrupulously) is quite a different thing. If I am trying to get someone to do something that they have no desire or willingness to do I am not motivating, I am manipulating, and if they do whatever I'm attempting to manipulate them into doing it is not due to their motivation, but rather to my manipulation; which is *controlling*, not motivating. Too often in youth work we focus on manipulating young people into doing that which we think they should do rather than creating conditions that motivate their desire and willingness.

There are six conditions that create internal motivation, which I not-so-cleverly have dubbed the Six Keys to Motivation. See Appendix B for a description of the Six Keys.

The Second Support: Failure

By far, the most difficult support for a youth worker to provide is allowing a young person to fail. Even if we understand how important failure is; even if we communicate that to a young person and encourage them to do things where failure is not only possible, but likely; actually stepping back and allowing them to experience failure can be the most heart-wrenching and emotionally painful experience a youth worker endures. The only thing that makes it tolerable is the knowledge that failure cannot be avoided. We may be able to postpone failure, but we cannot eliminate it.

The bane of all youthwork is recidivism, a term that is most common in justice systems referring to a return to criminal activity. But recidivism is a concern in all forms of youth work, as it describes a relapse into a previous condition or mode of behavior. A student who began to take their studies seriously may recidivate to a lack of interest. A drug user who has stopped using may recidivate to drug use (more commonly called "relapse"). A homeless youth who has secured shelter or housing may recidivate to homelessness. Whatever form of treatment we provide to a young person in order to change their behavior or circumstances may be undermined by recidivism; that is, a return to the behaviors, beliefs, or circumstances that we've worked so hard to help them overcome. I don't have the research to back this up, but I do have anecdotal observation from over 40 years of experience in the field to believe that recidivism is at least in part the result of discouraging and disallowing failure and enabling success (and I use enabling here in its negative social service connotation). A young person who is screwing up, making mistakes, and failing while in our care doesn't always look good for the class or program, but is very likely to internalize the class/program lessons and avoid recidivism upon leaving. On the other hand, a young person whose success has been enabled by the class/program, while they look very good while in our care, is more likely to demonstrate recidivist behavior upon exit.

Take a youth who needs employment, for example. The outcome desired is for the young person to obtain a job. One program does this by supporting the youth's *efforts*, while the second program supports a youth's *outcomes*. In the "effort" program, staff provides information and guidance and supports the youth's actions toward employment. The young person may fail to get interviews, or screw the interviews up, or get a job and lose it; maybe several times. Eventually, however, they learn how to be employable, and are able to seek and maintain employment in the future based on their experience in the program. In the "enable" program, staff works with employers to modify their expectations of a young person and give the youth "a chance" at employment. Staff supports that outcome by working with the employer and the young person to ensure success, helping the youth to get up on time, providing transportation to the job, and intervening with the employer when there are conflicts. Eventually the program supports are no longer there (all youth are in our care only temporarily) and, since the young person has mostly learned how to function within a highly enabling environment, they now have to begin the process on their own, where they may fail to get interviews, or screw the interviews up, or get a job and lose it, maybe several times.

Recidivism is made more likely by the postponement of failure. The skill of embracing failure is geared toward ensuring that the inevitable failures a youth must experience are experienced by the youth while *in our care* with the support of adults, rather than enabling a youth's success and ensuring that the youth will have to learn the lessons of failure at a later date, without our support … which we will then call "recidivism." *An Outlook on Outcomes* in Appendix C explores this concept further.

The Third Support: Reflection

In the 1960's movie classic "Dr. Strangelove," as the United States is about to unintentionally drop an atomic bomb on Russia, the Russian ambassador reveals that they have a "Doomsday Machine" that will destroy the world if they are bombed. Dr. Strangelove observes "Of course, the whole point of a Doomsday Machine is lost if you keep it a secret!" Similarly, the whole point of failure is lost if you don't reflect on it and learn the lessons that can be applied to the next effort. Edison didn't say "Results? Who needs results? Failure is its own reward!" He said that he got results every time because he discovered something else that wouldn't work. Making the same effort and experiencing the same failure over and over again is Einstein's definition of insanity; doing the same thing and expecting different results. The whole point of failure is to *learn* something, and to apply that knowledge to the next effort. Repeated failure is only a problem if you are repeating the exact same effort without applying knowledge gleaned from past efforts.

Think of failure as geodes. They're just your basic-looking unattractive sedimentary rocks until you crack them open and find that they contain stunning beauty. I was originally going to go with Tootsie Roll Pops for this analogy, until I remembered that Tootsie Roll Pops are delicious on the outside, too. But even Tootsie Roll Pops could be applicable when you consider that you don't get the goodie in the center until you've done the work of licking the candy coating, just as you don't get to see the beauty inside of a geode until you've done the work of cracking it open. Failure is like that; unattractive and unrewarding until you do the work of reflecting on the failure and discovering the lesson it has for you. That's when failure becomes a geode, or the yummy, chewy center of a Tootsie Roll Pop.

Failure is a gift, but you have to unwrap it, and that's the role of a youth worker; encourage effort that may result in failure (*because* it may result in failure), then help a young person unwrap the gift that failure contains. But be aware that this is not a case of us telling the young person what the gift is. If we respond to failure by pointing out all the things we think they did wrong, we are not embracing failure; we are lecturing and possibly berating. Our job is to help them realize that failure is a gift and encourage and support them in discovering what that gift is. We do that through reflection techniques; paraphrasing, listening, and approaches such as Motivational Interviewing. We don't get stuck on a young person's failure, but instead use failure as our signal to provide the "reflection" support.

The Fourth Support: Growth

We encourage a young person to take risks and make efforts (the first support). We allow and embrace failure (the second support). We help young people to reflect on and learn from failure (the third support). The only thing left to do now is to provide the fourth support and help the young person grow from the lessons learned. How do we do that? By starting the process all over again, with one difference. Having learned from their past failure they are now starting from a different place, and their next effort will be based on the lessons learned from their last failure. It is living out the old saying; I did the best I could with what I knew at the time, and when I learned how to do better, I did that.

Of course, having learned from past failure and starting the process over does not mean that they will now succeed. It's possible, perhaps even likely, that they will fail again; differently this time, but maybe equally spectacularly. We as youth workers now need to keep two things in mind. First, this is a new ball game. As long as they are reflecting on and growing from their previous failures, it doesn't matter if they fail again; perhaps even over and over and over. Maybe it will take them 5,126 designs to create their vacuum cleaner, or 9,000 experiments to fully understand what doesn't work. It doesn't matter to us. As long as they keep making efforts based on the lessons learned from previous attempts, we're good, and we're going to hang in there with them providing the Four Supports.

The second thing to keep in mind is to be realistic about our expectations of "success." In most cases where a young person is in the care of non-parental adults, our ultimate goal is to help them achieve legal, healthy, and self-supporting independence. Teachers may be focused on the educational and socialization piece of that goal; juvenile justice staff may be focused on the legal behavior piece of that goal; and outreach workers may be focused on the meeting basic needs and housing piece of that goal; but the ultimate goal is an independent young person who does not need program support and assistance. Now, just for a moment, let's consider parenting as an 18 year "program" for a young person. This young person is provided with 18 years of stable housing with their basic needs more than adequately met. They are loved and supported for those 18 years, with their medical, nutritional, and educational needs fully provided for. When they complete that "program" on their 18th birthday they are fully capable of moving out on their own into stable housing, with employment sufficient to support themselves independently … right?

I don't have to tell many parents the silliness of that assumption. Few young people, even with everything going for them, are actually capable of full independence on their 18th birthday. In fact, the last time it was studied, the National Longitudinal Survey of Youth 1997 discovered that most children don't leave home until they are in their 20's, and 1 in 5 were still dependent on home at the age of 27. There is little in the youth service field to indicate that this statistic has improved since 1997.

Remember that we are talking about young people from stable, supportive families that have everything going for them. That rarely describes who youth workers are actually working with. Our youth may have been abused or abandoned, in conflict with the law, homeless or otherwise deprived of basic needs, may be suffering from mental or physical disorders, drug use, or a host of other barriers or obstacles. And we're in their lives for a few months or a few years; nowhere near the 18-year-to-life support of a stable family. The fact is, we often expect youth who have been challenged beyond what any child should ever have to deal with to achieve goals and lifestyles in their teens, sometimes their early teens, that young people who have had everything they need for healthy development may not be able to achieve until their mid-late 20's.

Think about it. Do you still live in the same place you first moved to as a teen? Likely not, so what do we mean by "permanent housing?" Do you still have the very first job you ever worked? Again, likely not, so what do we mean by "permanent employment?" The fact is, we are not in the "outcome" business; we are in the "process" business. If a young person leaves our care better prepared for life than they were when they entered our care, that's "success;" even if they still have a way, perhaps a long way, to go.

The fifth of the Five Skills is:

The ability to embrace failure as a constituent part of the Four Supports to Success; Effort, Failure, Reflection, and Growth.

SUMMING UP

And now, the entire book in one quick summary, worded to be read and re-read as a personal reminder.

My work with young people is most effective when it rests on the foundation of five core competencies, or skills. Whenever I am in a professional relationship with a young person, I remember that ...

... treating young people respectfully is what I do, and it is not affected by or dependent on what young people do.

I have the skill to consistently treat young people in my care respectfully (verb); regardless of whether their behaviors, choices, and actions have earned my respect (noun), and regardless of whether they respect me, or are treating me respectfully. I consistently practice honesty, fairness, kindness, consideration, reliability, and concern through all of my words and actions.

... *what* I do is important, but *how* I do it is even more important.

I have the skill to establish therapeutic alliances with young people in which they feel safe, are able to trust, and have a role to play. I use the therapeutic alliance to create a resilience-fostering environment, and I recognize that I am a temporary and small part of a young person's life. *How* I spend my time with them is defined by a therapeutic alliance where I intentionally utilize every moment of my limited time with young people creating environments and experiences that serve to reduce and heal trauma and foster resilience, within the confines of and in fidelity with *what* I am doing (my job duties and the outcomes I am seeking).

… communication is the *means*, but the *end* I'm seeking is to understand and to be understood.

I have the skill to communicate cross-culturally with young people, and I pay attention to the impact of literalness, word interpretation, present-orientation, and power imbalance. I am consistent in my focus on understanding and being understood and I am always aware that young people communicate differently than adults.

… I'm going to react, but I'll *choose* to respond.

I have ability to recognize my reactions, interrupt them, and replace them with professional responses. I accept responsibility for my reactions and apologize, if needed when I do react. If I am unsure of how to professional respond, I default to empathy.

… failure is an important and necessary part of a young person's success.

I have the skill to embrace failure as a constituent part of the Four Supports to Success; Effort, Failure, Reflection, and Growth.

If I can start with respect, remember that it 'Tain't What You Do (It's the Way That You Do It) and that it 'Tain't What You Sing (It's the Way That You Sing It), respond rather than react, and embrace failure, the rest of my knowledge, skills and abilities will rest on a firm foundation of core competencies for youth work.

APPENDIX A
What versus How

In chapter two I described a difference between *what* we do and *how* we do it, but this not only describes the distinction between the job we have and the relationship that we need to establish, it is also a helpful treatment technique for addressing a youth's need to be *seen*; that is, to be acknowledged as a unique individual with value who has a meaningful role in a therapeutic alliance.

The way it works in practice is to clearly draw a distinction between *what* needs to be done (e.g., what is to be addressed; what is to be achieved), and *how* it needs to be done. *What* needs to be done is determined by job descriptions, funding, terms of probation, education goals; in other words, the reason why a therapeutic alliance exists, and the positive outcomes the relationship serves to achieve. But *how* these things are done is an area that can and should involve, or be determined by, the young person.

For example, a residential program I operated required that the program be kept clean by the residents themselves. Standards of cleanliness, and the need to have residents involved in maintaining those standards as part of their Independent Living education, were determined by the program, as that was *what* needed to be done. But there was no program-mandated manner in which these standards of cleanliness needed to be maintained, nor were there program-mandated consequences for not achieving and maintaining standards of cleanliness, beyond the possible consequence of program closure if we failed our city-mandated sanitation inspections. Methods and consequences were the responsibility of the residents themselves. In other words, what we did in terms of standards of cleanliness was mandated by the program; how we meet those standards of cleanliness was the responsibility of the residents. They could (and often did) decide to alter or change how they were maintaining standards of cleanliness and what the consequences were to residents who ignored their responsibilities ... the only thing that they couldn't do was decide that standards of cleanliness need not be met.

A 3rd grade teacher friend of mine described using "what versus how" in her classroom recently. A section of the curriculum required that her students begin to develop research skills. That was *what* needed to be done. But she allowed her students to determine *how* it was to be done, and they decided that they wanted to learn more about programs for and the needs of homeless youth. By allowing them to choose the *how*, they learned the *what* in a way that capitalized on their interests.

What versus How is applicable to almost any situation, at least to a limited degree. The more we are able to divide responsibilities in a therapeutic alliance into *what* needs to be done versus *how* it is going to be done, the greater will be the meaningful participation of the young person in the alliance. Whenever there is a "what" that a young person is required to do, grant them the authority over "how" it is going to be done.

APPENDIX B
The Six Keys to Motivation
Adapted by JT Fest from the work of Brooke Broadbent, with original content

The Six Keys to Motivation are presented here under the acronym "BICEPS" as a memory aid. BICEPS stands for Benefits, Importance, Clarity, Enjoyment, Positivity, and Success.

The First Key: Benefits

We can love this about ourselves or hate this about ourselves, but the fact remains that human beings are motivated to do things that they believe will benefit them personally. This reality has come to be known as the "WIIFM" Principle, or "What's In It For Me?" It sounds selfish, but it's really a neutral principle that results in acts, some of which may be selfish, some of which may be selfless. A mother sacrificing her life to save the life of her child might be considered a selfless act, but it is simply an example of the WIIFM Principle in action. What was in it for that mother? The life of her child, which she deemed of greater importance to her than her own life. To let her child die when she could save the child by dying herself would work against what she personally desired, and her child lived because the mother was motivated to action by how that action benefitted her personally.

In order for a young person to be motivated, they not only have to understand how an action will benefit them personally, but they also have to *desire* those benefits; and this is where youth workers often get frustrated with young people. Sometimes the benefits of an action are clear and undeniable. There's no dispute that completing one's basic education has benefits that are clear and easily documented, so we spend our time helping the young person understand those benefits, only to be angered by and frustrated with the young person when they remain unmotivated to go to school. The problem is that we are looking at it from *our* perspective and, even if the young person clearly understands the benefits that we are championing, we have not considered the young person's perspective on the benefits of *not* going to school, which are often current benefits versus long-term benefits. Young people, in no small part because of the fact that the prefrontal cortex of their brain (responsible for executive functions) is not yet fully developed, tend to be present-oriented and poor long-term thinkers. If, from the young person's perspective, the current benefits of not going to school are more desirable in the moment than are the benefits of completing their education, then even if they understand the benefits of going to school they will likely choose to not go to school. This is not a case of them being "unmotivated;" they are extremely motivated to not go to school. It's simply a case of them not being motivated to do what *we* think they should do, and instead being motivated to do something that *they* desire more than what we think they *should* desire.

To help young people become motivated we have to look at things from their perspective. Maybe they don't see the benefits of completing their education as greater than the benefits of not going to school right now. Fine. If our goal is to get them back into school, we need to sell it based on something that they do desire … socialization, certain opportunities available to students, sports, whatever. The point is to stop pushing the benefits that *we* desire for them, and instead push the benefits that *they* desire for themselves. No one has ever been motivated by what they *should* do or *must* do. Motivation comes from what one *wants* to do because of the benefits they see to themselves.

The Second Key: Importance

I'm not talking about a subjective judgement on how important or unimportant an action is, I'm talking about a feeling of personal importance; the feeling one has about one's *own* value or importance to others or events. We are far more motivated to do things where we feel that we specifically are necessary to that action. I am not likely to be greatly motivated to do something that anyone can do (or, if I am, importance is not the key that motivates me). But I will very likely be motivated to do something if I feel that I am personally important or necessary to the outcome, and where I feel valued for my (again, specific) participation.

From a Youth Development perspective, this directly relates to the protective factor of Meaningful Participation, and highlights one of the benefits of Youth/Adult Partnerships. It also speaks to the effectiveness of the therapeutic alliance. In any partnership or alliance, each person in the partnership/alliance has responsibilities that are necessary to the success of that partnership/alliance. Each individual is uniquely important and cannot be replaced without changing the nature of the partnership/alliance. I have to show up and participate; I can't not show up or send someone in my stead without affecting the nature of the partnership/alliance. Knowing this, I will be far more motivated to participate than I will be if my personal presence is not required.

Creating this key to motivate young people is a matter of creating roles and opportunities for young people in which *they as individuals* are important to the outcome and communicating their importance to them. To be clear, however, it is not simply saying that they are important; they have to have roles and responsibilities where they actually *are* important.

The Third Key: Clarity

Two things that can be the death knell to motivation are ambiguity (inexact or open to more than one interpretation) and/or vagueness (lack of certainty of distinctness). While often thought of as synonyms they are not quite the same thing. Something that is ambiguous is open to more than one distinct interpretation, where as something that is vague has no distinct interpretation. In both cases, however, what makes them problematic is that they both are the result of a lack of *clarity*.

The mark of clarity is that it is coherent (logically consistent), intelligible (comprehendible and able to be understood), certain (known for sure and beyond doubt), and definite (clearly stated or decided). Clarity is the antithesis of ambiguity and vagueness, and while clarity alone may not be a source of motivation, a lack of clarity will serve as a *deterrent* to motivation. In that respect, clarity may be thought of as a "reverse key." Its presence may not motivate, but its absence will demotivate.

Understanding this key underscores the importance of mastering the Third Skill: *'Tain't What You Sing (It's the Way That You Sing It).* The communication pitfalls discussed in that chapter are not only problematic in assuring that we understand and are understood, they are also responsible for demotivating young people in that they create ambiguity and vagueness. Forgetting to pay attention to "the way that you sing it" is not only responsible for misunderstandings, it can also be responsible for young people not being motivated to try to understand.

Communicating clearly is in and of itself one of the 5 most important core competencies for youth workers to develop, and it is also one of the 6 keys to creating environments that motivate.

The Fourth Key: Enjoyment

I have a friend who was working a full-time factory job. He hated it. He had to get up at 6 am to be on time for his 7 am shift, and he complained about it ad nauseam. He had trouble waking up on time every work day, and he'd groggily drag himself out of bed and practically sleepwalk to his job. Do you want to guess what he did on Saturdays? If you guessed "sleep in," you wouldn't even be close to being right. On most Saturdays he'd hop out of bed bright eyed and bushy-tailed at 4 am ... 2 full hours earlier than for his job ... in order to engage in one of his favorite pastimes; fishing. His problems with getting up at 6 for his job had nothing to do with the hour; it had to do with his motivation to work a factory job. Just as his lack of problems with bouncing out of bed even earlier had nothing to do with the hour; it had to do with his motivation to go fishing. It's as simple as this; he enjoyed fishing, so he was motivated to get up at 4. He did not enjoy working the factory job, so he was not motivated to get up a 6. He forced himself to get up at 6, however, because he enjoyed having money, so he was at least motivated enough by his desire for a paycheck to go to the job (but not enough to do so without complaint).

This key can be used two ways. The first is to find things that a young person enjoys doing and build activities around them. Does the young person like to be outside? Find ways to accomplish needed tasks that have the young person outdoors as much as possible. Do they enjoy being alone? Find ways to accomplish needed tasks that they can do mostly on their own. You get the idea; there is always more than one means to an end, select the means that involves the greatest amount of things that a young person enjoys, and they will be far more motivated than if all they perceive is drudgery. The second way to use this is to make things they don't enjoy enjoyable. Make it fun. Use humor. Include people and things that they enjoy being around. Young people can be motivated to do the most boring, mundane tasks if they enjoy the people they are doing it with or the places they are doing them.

The Fifth Key: Positivity

It's a simple formula; people are motivated by positive environments, and they are demotivated by negative environments. Even more to the point, people are motivated to be in positive environments and are not motivated to be in negative environments. You can test this one out yourself. Pay attention to different environmental situations in your life and give them each a "positivity score" based on the type of imagery, attitude, and feedback that you experience in each of them. Now give them each another score based on how willing, eager, and likely you are to place yourself in that environment if given a choice, and also how motivated to participate and how productive you think you are when in that environment. I suspect that you are going to see a direct correlation between your assessment of how positive an environment is, and your motivation related to that environment. But I submit that it is not simply correlation; it is causation. People are motivated by positive environments, positive thoughts, and positive feedback.

It's important to realize that "environment" is not a static concept. Yes, an environment that is "positive" when it is clean, functional, well organized, nicely decorated, and presents positive messages, but more than anything, an environment is the *people* in it, and people's relationship to the environment changes depending on their present circumstances. Consider a young person living in a transitional living program. The circumstance of the young person's life becomes part of that environment, as does the adult youth worker's responses to the young person's current circumstances. For example, a young person successfully completes their basic education and comes back to the program clutching their new High School Diploma. The program, as always, is clean, functional, well organized, nicely decorated, and presents positive messages. But in addition, the staff response is excited, congratulatory, and oozing compliments and acknowledgement. That routine positive environment has just been kicked up to a super-positive one where the young person feels great and is likely motivated to pursue further achievements. Now consider the exact same situation, except this time the young person is returning after an unsuccessful venture; they got turned down for or perhaps fired from a job, or they failed a test important to completing their education. Everything's the same, except the staff response. There's no excitement, no congratulations, no compliments or acknowledgement. Instead, the young person walks into dispassion, grief, criticism, and admonition. The facility is still clean, functional, well organized, nicely decorated, and filled with positive messages, but this routine positive environment will be perceived by the young person as one that is negative, due to the staff's response, and the young person will be unlikely to be motivated to try something else where they might also fail, because they've learned that failure creates a negative environment.

So, what am I saying? That we're supposed to be all excited and congratulatory and heap compliments and acknowledgement on young people when they screw up or fail? Well, yeah, sort of. I mean, it's not about faking positivity about negative actions or results in a young person's life. But it is about our *attitude* toward failure, and whether or not we truly believe and accept that failure is a necessary prerequisite to success. Our job then becomes to identify and focus on the positive aspects of the failure and responding to those aspects with positivity. Our actions in these situations should always be geared toward the impact they will have on the young person's future efforts. Think about it this way. The recent high school grad who experiences negative responses to their achievement will not be motivated to achieve more, but if they experience positive responses, they will be. The opposite is also true. The young person who screws up and receives negative responses to their failure will not be motivated to risk failing again in pursuit of success, but if they experience positive responses, they will be.

Promoting positivity is what we as professionals do to encourage success, and it should not be dependent on the actions of a young person.

One final thought. We shouldn't wait for positive events to provide positive acknowledgment. I once wrote a newspaper article about an experience I had at the Los Angeles airport. An old man was shuffling along and I noticed that he'd dropped his ticket. No one else seemed to notice, so I got up, ran over to pick up his dropped ticket, and then caught up and gave it to him. I didn't think anyone had seen me do that, but when I turned around to return to my seat I saw a janitor who was going through the concourse with a trash can cleaning things up. He obviously had seen the entire event, because he *caught my eye, smiled at me, and nodded.* It was a small gesture of acknowledgement; a small gesture of approval from a stranger in an airport concourse … but I instantly felt like a million bucks. All it took was that one person recognizing and acknowledging my deed to give my actions validation, and to give me the unequaled positive feeling of having done a good deed.

Acknowledgement is powerful, but acknowledgement is not always positive. One can acknowledge people's deficits and screw ups … and we do that all the time with young people. We correct their behaviors, we set limits, we point out their negative attitudes and actions; we negatively acknowledge them nearly every day. I'm not saying it's malicious on our parts … it's often part of the job. But that just underscores the critical need to put as much emphasis ... ideally *more* emphasis ... on positive acknowledgement. We are trained to see when young people are pushing boundaries or limits and to intervene, but do we put as much effort into catching them doing things that are good and right, and noticeably giving them acknowledgement for those behaviors, as well? An environment where we feel acknowledged for that which is positive is a motivating environment, and one where we are likely to wish to spend our time.

The Sixth Key: Success

When speaking of "success" as a key to motivation, we are not referring to goal attainment or specific achievements. Instead, we are speaking of feelings of competence and accomplishment resulting from any outcome; be it a desired or an undesired one.

Let's say I set out to hike to the top of a steep trail. A quarter of the way up I realize that I should have brought more water and a few energy snacks. Halfway up my shoes are giving me blisters and I'm huffing and puffing from being too out of shape. Two thirds of the way up the weather changes and I find myself unprepared for the cold wind and rain, so I quit and take my hungry, thirsty, blistered, out-of-shape, cold and wet body back down the trail to my car.

Have I failed? I suppose one could look at it that way as I didn't achieve my goal of making it to the top of the trail. But think of all I did achieve. I now know how much water and food I need to take with me; I know that I'll need different shoes for the hike, that I need to get myself into somewhat better physical condition to attempt a climb like that, and that I need to be better prepared for changing weather conditions as I climb. This morning when I set out I only knew what my goal was; this evening as I nourished myself, shopped for shoes, made a plan to improve my physical endurance, and packed a hiking bag with weather gear, I knew how I was going to achieve that goal. Today's hike may have left me weak, blistered, exhausted, and cold, but it was not a failure. As Edison would say, I now knew what didn't work, giving me the knowledge I need to make it to the top of that trail. That's success. I accomplished something ... not my goal, but I learned what I need to obtain my goal; and with that knowledge I feel competent to try again.

As long as an effort results in accomplishment (even if it wasn't the accomplishment being sought) and an increase in competence, we're speaking about success, not failure. And as long as a young person is aware of their accomplishment and competence it will serve as an internal motivator for continued effort.

APPENDIX C
An Outlook on Outcomes
The impact of what we measure
I originally published this article in 2014

All too often we are giving young people cut flowers
when we should be teaching them to grow their own plants
~ John W. Gardner

I strongly suspect we can all agree that outcomes are important. When I present the Youth Development approach I describe outcomes as the "bottom line" of youth work. No matter how you work with young people, the value of your work can only be measured in relationship to what results from your work.

I also suspect that the fact that outcomes are important may be the only area on which we can all agree. Agreeing that outcomes are important doesn't help us to reach consensus on what types of outcomes are important, and it certainly doesn't help us determine the most effective ways to measure success in reaching specific outcomes.

This creates a situation where we may not agree on what we do agree is the most important aspect of our work. To make matters worse, we rarely even get to debate outcomes because, more often than not, outcomes are decided for us.

For the majority of youth services, the basis of support is a third-party contract. A private or public source provides the financial support for delivery of the service to the consumer. This sets up an awkward situation right off the bat, as the *consumer* of the service is not the *customer*, and it is the customer who gets to determine outcomes.

When the customer is not the consumer it directly impacts the manner in which outcomes are viewed. For example, let's say I am a customer who is paying a food service to provide daily meals to one thousand people. I'm sure I would be concerned that the meals meet minimal nutritional standards, and I'd also be concerned about the cost of providing the meals. But let's say instead that I'm paying the service to provide meals to my family and myself. While I may still be concerned about minimal standards and cost-effectiveness, I'm likely to be more concerned about the health and nutrition of the meals beyond minimal standards, the quality of the ingredients, the taste and variety of the menu, and my family's specific culinary likes and dislikes. The simple reality is that outcomes will be different depending on whether the customer is also the consumer.

This reality points out a major problem with the current state of many youth outcome requirements. As they have been developed by customers who are not consumers, there is a strong influence on cost-effectiveness -- in my opinion to the detriment of other more critical outcomes from the perspective of a young person's needs and development. This problem is compounded by a simple fact: young people are not cost-effective.

Need proof? Have a child -- but that might be more than you're willing to invest in this exercise. So instead consider this. According to the United States Department of Agriculture (2013 figures), raising a child from birth through age 17 will cost $241,080.001. That's over $13,393.00 every year, for 18 years. After investing these multiple tens of thousands of dollars, you have bought yourself an 18-year-old ready for college. That means more investment. Even a standard 4-year bachelor's degree will cost at minimum about $35,000 and can cost upwards of $120,000 or more -- and that may be just for tuition. Associated costs can easily run you several grand more a year.

When all is said and done, be prepared to sink somewhere between three hundred thousand and half a million dollars into your child. If that financial investment has resulted in an average American child, you now face a 1 in 4 possibility that they will continue to live with you until they are 34.

Now let's consider an example from the youth work field. For this example I'll stick to an area that I'm familiar with; transitional living programs (TLP's) for street-dependent youth. In a TLP we basically have the same responsibility as parents. The young person is living at the program 24/7 and all of their needs are being provided for by the program or through the program's resources. If we use the previously stated numbers, we can expect to spend $13,393.00 per year on each resident and, since a parent's time is not included in this figure, this does not include personnel and administrative costs. Therefore, annually a 7-bed facility can expect to spend $93,751.00 in addition to the cost of personnel and administration. Since conservatively these latter costs generally represent 70% and 10% of a TLP's budget respectively, a 7-bed TLP should be funded at about $468,755.00.

There are several things to consider about this figure. The first is that no federal TLP in the nation receives this level of funding. $200,000.00 is the maximum, and many TLP's receive far less. Consider also that, even if a program were receiving the $468,755.00 figure, we are talking about salaries in the $25,000.00 - $35,000.00 range -- salaries which are simply not sufficient to compensate and retain quality employees considering the level of skill required by the program. But that's only the beginning of the story.

Remember that our dollar figures are based on the expenses required by a healthy adolescent who has been raised in a secure, caring family that continues to provide a basis of support. This does not describe the situation of the adolescent we see in programs for at-risk youth. The adolescent we see often has medical and mental health needs that are not considered in the "standard" cost of raising a child. They are often developmentally delayed, lacking adequate support systems and socialization skills, and suffering post-traumatic stress from abuse, neglect, and abandonment.

So, all of this considered, we have a situation where outcomes are dictated by a customer who is not a consumer, predicated on cost-effectiveness with a population that is not cost-effective, and applied to consumers who have greater challenges and obstacles than their peers who end up hanging out at their parent's house until they're 34 and are able to finally figure out what they want to be when they grow up.

As stated at the beginning of this article, though, outcomes are important -- regardless of how they are measured they are the "bottom line" of what we do. And, despite my treatise on cost-effectiveness, customers (funding sources) need to determine if they are getting their money's worth. I fully understand this reality, and I have been in social services long enough to know that there can be a tremendous amount of waste. I'm actually a rather big "accountability" kind of guy. My concern is not with measurement per se. Rather it is with what we chose to measure and the effects of our choices.

Outcome categories

The three primary categories that all outcomes can be placed in are achievement, prevention, and developmental. Achievement outcomes are tangible accomplishments; e.g., completing school, getting a job, finding stable housing. Prevention outcomes are avoidance of problem behaviors; e.g., pregnancy, drug abuse, violence. Developmental outcomes are beliefs, behaviors, knowledge, and skills; e.g., self-worth, responsibility, autonomy, employability.

It should be clear from these definitions why the overwhelming majority of outcomes required by funding sources fall into the achievement and prevention categories. If you are counting the pennies you invest and looking at what you're buying, it is natural to focus on accomplishments and preventing problems; to focus on things we want young people to do or the things we don't want them to do (or both). These aren't bad things. Young people completing school, getting jobs, avoiding early pregnancy, and staying away from violence and drugs -- who can argue with these outcomes? Certainly not me, and my caution is not about the outcomes themselves ... it is about focusing on them.

There is a law that rears its ugly head from time to time with which I'm sure many of you have had personal experience. It is not a human law, it is a natural law, making it all that more difficult to avoid. I'm referring to the Law of Unintended Consequences, and the truly devious aspect of this law is that it tends to hide behind good intentions. This is why debate is so critical in our field, because everything we do is based in good intentions, but good intentions are not enough -- we also have to have good results. As mentioned earlier in this article we rarely debate outcomes. We more often than not simply try to achieve what our customers are purchasing, and in so doing we unleash the Law of Unintended Consequences on our young consumers.

Focusing on achievement and prevention outcomes completely misses the point of what young people need. Do the young people you work with need jobs, or education, or housing? Do they need to avoid pregnancy, or violence, or drugs? Before you answer "yes" consider the following.

Imagine that a young person has developed beliefs and behaviors that demonstrate personal well-being and a sense of connection and commitment to others. They think of themselves as a "good" person with something of value to contribute, and they feel that they are succeeding in life. They feel safe in the world and can create a personal structure that makes daily events somewhat predictable. They are able to exercise some control over their lives and are accountable for their actions. They are able to differentiate themselves while maintaining attachment to community and higher beliefs and principles.

Now also imagine that they possess knowledge and skills that give them the ability and motivation to ensure current and future success. They have the ability to gain the necessary skills for employment, and they are able to learn, think, problem-solve, and study independently. They respect differences among groups and individuals and are able to work collaboratively and sustain relationships. Additionally, they are motivated to ensure current and future physical health and know how to cope with situations and engage in leisure and fun.

Would you need to find this imagined youth a job? Would you need to get them off of drugs, or deal with their issues of violence? Would you need to encourage them to finish school? Probably not, because the young person I described is unlikely to be engaging in risk behaviors and is motivated to complete school and find employment on their own.

The above description represents the outcomes we look for in young people when we focus on their development. When focusing on developmental outcomes we don't need to focus on achievement and prevention because such things are a natural consequence of a young person's healthy development. In fact, it's not that achievement and prevention is unimportant, it's that it is too important to make it the focus of our work because, when we do, we open the door for the Law of Unintended Consequences.

Unintended consequences of achievement and prevention

No outcomes are easier to obtain than achievement and prevention. This is a problem, because the easier they become, the greater the disservice we do to the young people with whom we work. Let me correct myself just slightly. It's not that achievement and prevention outcomes are easy, it's that there are shortcuts; easy ways to their realization. For example; do you want to get a young person off of drugs? Easy. Lock him or her up for 30 days. Goal accomplished, they're off drugs. Of course, whether or not they stay off drugs after release is a huge question, but the program may have successfully accomplished its fundable goal. How about securing employment for a young person? Easy. Locate a job and place your young person in the position. Goal accomplished, they're employed. Of course, within a week they may tell the boss to stick it where the sun don't shine and rejoin the ranks of the unemployed, but, again, the program may have accomplished its fundable goal.

These two examples highlight the potential problem with tying funding to achievement and prevention outcomes. It provides incentive for programs to take shortcuts in order to obtain the measurable outcome that justifies continued support. This is particularly true when we are trying to crank out short-term outcomes, such as taking a young person who is coming from an 18-year history of abuse, neglect, poverty, and educational failure and attempting to make them independent and self-supporting in weeks or months, years before their stable, healthy peers are able to accomplish the same outcome. The result is that we may be focused on meeting *our* needs to justify the dollars than we are on meeting the young person's developmental needs, and guess who loses in that scenario?

Why do we so often see young people as failures and incompetent? Why do we see high recidivism rates, and why does follow-up reveal such a high rate of inability to maintain successful outcomes? Could it be because we are pushing outcomes that are ahead of a young person's development? And could that be because we are pursuing the wrong types of outcomes to begin with?

Unfortunately, increased outcome dissatisfaction may give birth to responses that exasperate the problem. Such is the case with performance-based contracting. If you are not familiar, performance-based contracting is the idea that a program will receive a certain percentage of funding for providing services (it varies, but usually in the 60% to 70% range), and the remainder of the funding will only be paid based on outcome measurement -- the same achievement and prevention measurements the program was struggling to obtain under the old system of contracting. While the good intention here is to guarantee that services are working for young people, the whole concept is based on the faulty premise (in my opinion) that failure to obtain achievement and prevention outcomes in the short-term is a result of incompetent services. All performance-based contracting does is "up the ante" in terms of creating incentives for shortcuts, as well as increasing another unintended consequence of the achievement and prevention focus; creaming.

Creaming is the tendency of programs to gradually evolve to serving higher functioning youth. If a program must demonstrate short-term accomplishments in order to survive, it will naturally begin to serve only those young people who are developmentally able to succeed in the short-term. The more "difficult" youth eventually gets screened out of services because he or she needs too much or takes too long. The ultimate end result is that we are spending all of our dollars on youth who don't really need the help, and none of our dollars on those who do -- at least, none of our service dollars; we certainly still pay the tab in social and legal costs.

The irony is that, for all of our focus on cost-effectiveness, we end up with the most cost-ineffective system one could imagine, and we repeat this mistake in cycles. I have been around long enough to see grassroots services start up to meet the needs of the "difficult" and underserved youth, only to evolve to serving the higher functioning youth in order to demonstrate fundable outcomes. New grassroots agencies then appear to serve the more "difficult" youth the previous agencies used to serve. Throughout this process, young people who really need assistance are the ones least likely to get it.

A new outcome focus

I suggest that any attempts at outcome measurement and program accountability are doomed to failure until we change our outcome focus. To this end, I recommend two major shifts in outcome measurement and accountability.

1. Focus on development, not achievement or prevention

    I am a strong advocate of the Youth Development approach, mainly because it is research based, and it works. One of the primary tenets of this approach is that perceived problems are not the issue. Rather, "problems" are symptoms of unmet developmental needs. If this is true (and I propose that it is), then a problem-focus is just a symptom-focus ... what we need to do is to cure the disease. Outcome measurements, therefore, should not focus on the traditional jobs, education, and/or delinquent behaviors. They should instead focus on young people's development.

2. Measure the provider, not the consumer

Remember the customer/consumer separation discussed earlier? One difficulty affecting outcomes is that, in effect, we have the customer holding the employee (programs) accountable to the consumer's behavior. What makes better sense is for the customer to hold the employee accountable to its own behavior.

Resiliency research has shown that young people's development flourishes in an environment of Protective Factors, and we know that assisting a young person in their developmental process is the path to meaningful and lasting achievement and prevention outcomes. That being said, the customer should hold the employee accountable to the manner in which they are providing services. Instead of measuring a program's success by what young people are doing or not doing, success would be measured by what a program is doing or not doing, grounded in the research-based knowledge of how Protective Factor environments foster a young person's innate resilience, enabling them to accomplish achievement and prevention outcomes according to their capacity and developmental readiness rather than an artificial timeline based on meeting pre-determined outcome measurements.

Interestingly, using this approach, achievement and prevention outcomes could still be measured over time as an indicator of a program's long-term effectiveness, but the tie to funding would be on the program's activities rather than the young person's outcomes. This change in focus would free programs from the pressures that lead to creaming, shortcuts, and outright manipulation of outcome data, and allow them to focus instead on the specific developmental needs of the young people seeking their services.

Conclusion

Management consultant Peter Drucker once stated; "What gets measured gets done." If we measure our success by a youth's performance, we can expect programs to focus on performance above all else, resulting in the unintended consequences described above and ultimately failing the young people we serve. If we measure our performance based on researched and proven practice that we know meets the developmental needs of young people, then, ironically, we can expect to see greater success in reaching the achievement and prevention goals that we currently measure. Is such a change in focus likely to happen? Probably not, but that doesn't mean that it's not worth advocating.

ABOUT THE AUTHOR

JT (Jerry) Fest is the author of two previous books on working with young people; "Street Culture: an epistemology of street-dependent youth," and "The Winning Hand Workbook: Positive Youth Development in 6 Easy Lessons." He has been an advocate for young people since 1970, and founded and worked 12 years as the director of Janus Youth Program's Willamette Bridge -- a continuum of services including streetwork and outreach, emergency shelter, transitional living, independent living, case management, and youth business and partnership programs. In 1987 he developed the "self-government" model for residential services; one of the earliest program models based on the principles of Youth Development. In 1996 he received the Oregon Child and Youth Care Association "Citizen of the Year" award for his work with street-dependent youth, and received the Year 2000 Helen Reser Bakkensen award for *exemplary leadership, service, and advocacy on behalf of homeless youth.*

Made in the USA
San Bernardino, CA
26 February 2019